The knowledge in this book has been available
since the beginning of time.
It did not come *from* me. It came *to* me.
Let it bring freedom to budding swimmers
and to all people on the path.

Melon Dash
Walnut Creek, California, 2006

CONQUER YOUR FEAR OF WATER

An Innovative Self-Discovery Course in Swimming

By Melon Dash

authorHOUSE™

1663 LIBERTY DRIVE, SUITE 200
BLOOMINGTON, INDIANA 47403
(800) 839-8640
WWW.AUTHORHOUSE.COM

First published by AuthorHouse 5/22/06

ISBN: 1-4208-8539-1 (eb)
ISBN: 1-4208-6444-0 (sc)

Library of Congress Control Number: 2006904752

Printed in the United States of America
Bloomington, Indiana

This book is printed on acid-free paper.

Graphics by Melon Dash and Michelle Becker
Cover Design by David Arsenault
Photographs are of students in class by Melon Dash

TABLE OF CONTENTS

"This book is about healing fear. Melon Dash knows how to heal those hobbled by fear of water, deep or shallow, and bring the joy of swimming to all." —Cynthia Tuttelman, M.D.

"Dash is onto something big. Her system has affected the way I work with some of my clients." —Nancy Merz, Psychotherapist

"How does Melon teach people to overcome their fear in water, you ask? The most enjoyable, inspiring, and loving way you could possibly imagine." —Anonymous

"I can never, ever, ever thank you enough. Better than great. I cannot recommend it enough. It is truly a miracle." —Joe Baron, Stay-at-home Dad

"It truly is miracle swimming." —Claude Chavez, Plumber, and numerous others

"This book has more useful information about learning to swim than all the beginning swim classes I've taken in my whole life, combined. I've taken a lot of classes." —Deborah Kemper, Travel Writer

"This method cannot and does not fail." —Mary Alice Yund, Chemist

"I cannot begin to tell you how much I learned and how much more confident I now am in water. Your methods truly had a miraculous impact on me and my newfound confidence in water have opened doors that I thought would always remain shut." —Rich Kennedy, Department Manager

"This summer was truly one of the best summers I have ever had because of you and your phenomenal program."—Mark Volpicelli, The Converted Skeptic

As Seen on NBC News: Today ("The Today Show") and
CNN Headline News

ACKNOWLEDGEMENTS

First and foremost, many thanks to every student who has ever taken my classes, 2,800 of you since 1983, and the six in New Hampshire in 1978. You prodded me to learn all of the new information in this book.

Highest kudos and warmest gratitude go to my students who have become instructors: Fred Peoples, Jeannie Mariscal, and Richard Schwarzenberger.

Many, many thanks to all the volunteers who have assisted in my work: the spotters, the video shipper, and office assistants.

Thank you to each of the students who generously gave permission to have their photographs, stories, and quotes included in this book.

Many thanks also to each reader of my manuscript. Your enthusiasm and attentive feedback were invaluable!

Each team of you and me—reader and writer—is a steppingstone to the world's freedom in water and vast dissemination of this information to all who can benefit from it. Thank you for sharing this with me. Together, we can reach those goals.

Lastly, I wish to express my gratitude for the birth of print-on-demand books and the "e-book" for making "Conquer Your Fear of Water..." possible, for giving voice to new authors, and for their advantages over traditional books regarding the environment: only books that are ordered are printed.

PREFACE

If you knew that 2+2 equaled 4, and you saw the whole world adding 2+3, or 2+6 or 2+135 and trying to get 4, always coming up with an incorrect answer and basing further calculations on these answers, you might feel as I do: like shouting from the top of the Empire State Building with a megaphone, "Two plus two is four! I guarantee it. Let me show you. Then the rest of your calculations will be correct. Life will be easier. The world will be a better place!"

For twenty-three years this is how I've felt about teaching swimming (and assisting SCUBA diving classes) for adults who are afraid in water. Many teachers have been adding 2+3, or 2+6, or 2+149 and trying to get 4. It never equals 4. I was trained in the traditional method as a swimming instructor. When I asked myself why the training didn't work for my students who were afraid in water, the answer appeared right before my eyes. It was too good to keep to myself. My students and I believe it should be the new way beginning swimming is taught.

Two (an adult afraid in water) and two (the information in this book) is four: an adult who is confident, safe, and free in water and knows how to remain safe. It works every single time. That's the difference between this teaching and the traditional.

INTRODUCTION

> *"I love the water. It's the depth that gets me."*
> —Giselle

Have you taken swimming lessons and emerged without knowing how to swim? Have you decided not to take more lessons because you became discouraged? Have you been taught by youngsters who were inexperienced working with adults?

For a century, many adults have taken swimming classes that didn't meet them at their level. Their level hadn't been named. The name was "afraid." This was a level that preceded "Beginning Swimming" lessons but which has remained undefined until recently. May this book bring tremendous light to this once invisible stage of learning.

Overcoming fear is an intimate process. It takes place at the core of you. It requires slowing down and coming to a full stop. I hope you'll treat yourself with the utmost respect, compassion and patience. The journey is simple and clear. The process is predictable and reliable and fun. It just may involve something you never considered before.

Topics of overcoming fear and learning to swim are presented here as they usually come up in my classes. You *would not want to skip* steps in this book when you go to the pool.

By my definition, if you're uncomfortable in water, you're afraid of *something*. It makes complete sense to be afraid in water until you know how the water works and how to be in control in it. However, knowing how the water works and how to be in control in it have never been systematically taught in beginning swimming classes, to my knowledge.

You cannot reasonably expect yourself to succeed if you aren't taught how to be in control in water, if you aren't met at your level and your questions aren't answered. Would anyone expect a 5 year old to learn to read without learning the alphabet first?

In this book you'll find the steps to learning to swim and the answers to all the questions students ask as they engage in our classes, Miracle Swimming: New Lessons for Adults Afraid in Water. You'll see photographs of students learning skills in class. You'll be able to write your thoughts and answers in the book in response to the exercises given. You will surely come to a new understanding. It will turn your swimming around.

Here are the answers you've awaited for decades. Best wishes for your fun and new freedom.

Melon Dash

PART 1

HOW TO KNOW IF YOU'RE AFRAID IN WATER

Will this book help you?

Some people who are afraid in water are aware that they're afraid, and some are not. Students have said to me, "I'm not sure I'm afraid in water. But I do cling to the sides when I'm in the deep." To me, clinging to the sides in the deep means they're afraid.

Have you been unsuccessful learning how to tread water or how to breathe while swimming? Perhaps you believe it's because you haven't practiced enough or that you haven't been taught in a way you could understand. Those could be true. Or, it may be that you weren't in control.

If you're unsure that you can remain in control in the middle of the deep end of the pool, or swimming out to a raft in a lake and stopping to rest on the way, or at any point between the lawn chair and deep water, this book is written for you. Discomfort and uncertainty are two faces of fear. If you weren't afraid, you wouldn't hesitate to go to the raft—even if you didn't know strokes. If you have wished you could swim, or felt badly that you couldn't, rest assured: it's okay to be afraid in water. And there is a pleasant path out of fear to freedom.

> *Do you think that just because you can't swim, or because you panic in deep water, or you get water in your nose, or you can't open your eyes under water, or you sink, or you can't get a breath, or you didn't pass your swimming test...you weren't born a swimmer? Impossible. You were born with the blueprint to learn to swim, every bit as much as Mark Spitz, Janet Evans, and Ian Thorpe were. Soon, you'll know this, as well as I do.*

PART 2

THE URGENCY TO GET STARTED

Urgency is a common state but it impedes learning.
Here's what you can do about it.

How many years have you've longed to be free in water?
Number of years: _____

You may feel like skipping these pages and going directly to the steps of learning the skills. But understanding the material in the following pages is the first step.

Urgency is a desperate sense of wanting to be ahead of where you actually are. In a few pages, you'll find what happens inside us when we're ahead of ourselves. We need to become aware of this crucial state.

Wanting to be somewhere you're not:
your body is on the left. Your attention, you, are on the right.

For now, please feel the sensations of urgency if you have them—the hurry, internal speed, tension, excitement, wanting-to-get-this-part-over-with—and allow them to be there.

There are times when urgency is a useful thing. Learning to overcome fear and swim is *not* one of those times. When you engage in the learning process, the feeling of urgency can get in the way of learning. (It helps to get you started on the path, though.) If you feel urgent to learn, feel where urgency is in your body, stop reading, and experience it *fully*.

Why stop reading to experience it? Because when you become present to it, it has a chance to let go. When it does let go, then instead of your attention being focused on getting to the goal, all your attention will be available for learning. With all your attention available for learning, you can only succeed.

PART 3
WHAT HAPPENED?

You are not alone.
Basically the same thing happened to everyone who is afraid in water. It happened millions of ways, but there is a common thread among all of them.

Something made you afraid in water. For most people, it was a frightening experience in water or possibly out of the water. Also for most people, a parent was afraid in water or "didn't swim." For a few people, the cause of fear is unknown. Virtually always, there was a loss of control. This fear can be healed.

We'll spend more time on the specifics of what happened later in the book. Here is one sample of an early experience of an afraid student.

> *My fear of water began years ago, when as a child, a well-intentioned but uninformed swim teacher pushed me into the deep end of the pool, thinking this would get me to swim. Needless to say, he was mistaken. I went on to become an adult who loved water but never fully enjoyed being in water because I was always nervous and afraid. I've tried other classes since then. But it seemed as though I could never "get" the breathing, my arms and legs refused to work together, and the panic in my belly just wouldn't go away. Plus, the teacher usually wanted me to do things that I didn't feel ready to do. It was awful.*
>
> *The most important lesson TSI taught me is that when I take my time, going as slowly as I need to in order to feel safe and comfortable, I learn. I learn without fail, and with great joy.*
>
> *—Anonymous*

PART 4
WHAT DIDN'T HAPPEN?

Relieve the afraid student of a burden.
Explain why learning to swim hasn't worked yet.
Let afraid students know it wasn't their fault.

After you became afraid, you may or may not have tried to overcome it. What you needed was not what you found, however. Your questions may have gone unanswered. Perhaps you were given misinformation or learning-steps that were out of order.

$2+100 \neq 4$

Everyone can learn to swim. Yes, you. It's not that you can learn to swim if you grin and bear it. It's not that you can learn to swim if you feel the fear and do it anyway (though that approach has its place elsewhere). It's not that you can learn to swim if you force yourself. It's that you can learn to swim happily, gently, and predictably. There's no mystery about it...anymore.

If you've taken swimming lessons before and you haven't learned to swim or to breathe or to be comfortable in water shallow and deep, it's probably because you and the instructor were trying to add 2 and "not 2" to get 4. You were probably trying to add "you" plus "swimming mechanics" to get confidence. They don't add up.

Yes, you can make some progress in "swimming" lessons. But if you're afraid in water, the lessons fall short of what you need. However, if we add "you" to the full list of sequential steps of learning, it will add up to safety, freedom in water both shallow and deep, comfortable swimming, and skill in preventing panic. If you haven't yet reached your goals, you are like thousands of people nation- and worldwide who have asked me, "Will your lessons work for me?" In a word, yes.

It's not your instructor's fault that the lessons fell short. The instructors and the instructors' instructors were unaware that traditional lessons did not meet the safety standards of afraid students. Instructors thought they were doing the right thing.

In order to make all swimming students safe—as safe as they can be—instruction must dive to the depths of what safety really is. It's not simply, "Don't run on the deck. No horseplay. Only one person on the diving board at a time." Safety resides at a level never before, to my knowledge, examined by the swimming industry or perhaps any industry. This book teaches it. The details are not new: they are newly discovered.

It's okay to be afraid in water. In fact, most adults in America are. Many say, "I love the water." But put them into water over their heads in a pool, and 46% of them (92 million out of 200 million) are afraid. Put them in deep open water (lakes, oceans) and 64% are afraid. That's 128 million American adults. Ask them to put their heads under water and 39% are afraid (Gallup Poll, 1998). Yet all of them, and you, were born to be swimmers.

What is swimming, anyway? Is it perfect strokes even if done with fear? Is it getting from here to there in water but being unable to stop and rest in the middle?

I believe that swimming is not about doing a perfect stroke. My definition of swimming for the purposes of this course and my classes is confidence in water, especially deep water. Confidence in water automatically brings ease in water, being able to move from here to there without tiring, being free to play, and having a choice about what to do. It brings a curiosity about deep water: "Is the deep water the same as the shallow?" And in the answering of that question, a student learns that yes, it is. Only his mind is different in the deep. And that brings the question, "What shall I do about my mind in deep water?"

In my opinion, and in that of most of my students, if someone can do the crawl stroke in shallow water but not in deep water with confidence, he or she cannot really swim yet. He would say, "I can swim—sort of." To him, the term swimming includes not just mechanics, but also the component of confidence. Both are your birthright.

Everyone is born a swimmer. Everyone is born a talker and a walker, a reader and a driver. You weren't born knowing how to do these things already. You were born with the blueprint within you to learn them. You just needed the steps. You learned how to walk and talk beautifully because you didn't skip any steps. You learned to read and drive step by step. You didn't learn to swim because many steps were skipped. But when you skip no steps, you can't help but learn to swim.

If you're afraid in water and you're like the 2,800 adults I have worked with since 1983, you've felt frustrated and confined not to be able to learn to swim as you've wished. Perhaps it's felt embarrassing or shameful as well. My students say so. True, it has caused you to miss opportunities. You want to be free. There is a fun, easy way to heal your fear and become free in water.

If someone is afraid in water, there's an essential ingredient he needs before he can learn swimming mechanics. (When I use she or he, I mean both genders.) If it's not learned, the student won't learn to swim, period. Those people who already have it are the people who learn to swim.

That essential ingredient is control. Despite the fact that swimming has been taught to millions of people without teaching control, the method that was used was not based on universal principles that worked for all students. It has never worked for students who are afraid. Nor does it teach true safety. The millions of students who did learn to swim—became

9

confident in deep water—were in control. But the teaching method presumed that students were in control, and therefore control was never identified as Step 1.

2+2=4

YOU HAVE TO BE IN CONTROL TO LEARN TO SWIM.

And what is safety? Yes, it can be "no boats driving through the swim area." But this is not the primary safety you're concerned with. You're most concerned with the safety you'll feel if you're in control of yourself—if you know you won't panic.

Learning safety did not happen.

PART 5
HOW TO FIX IT

Teach how to overcome fear.
Provide the steps.
Provide the steps of learning to swim.
Lead students through the process of fixing it.

THE ELEVEN FRONTS OF FREEDOM IN WATER

A "front" is a leading edge. In overcoming fear in water, there are eleven
fronts on which you can make progress toward the goal of freedom in
deep water (eleven angles from which to approach it). Each is part of the
whole picture. When you've reached your limit of what's fun on one front,
you can turn to another front and continue to make progress. Progress on
one front builds confidence, which enhances your progress on all fronts.
Resting often brings up the rear on each front as well. The fronts are:

- Presence, control and internal speed
- Your face
- On your front
- On your back
- Spirituality of learning
- Fun
- Propulsion
- Breath
- Being vertical
- Water entries
- Deep water

In each of these areas there is a sequence of steps which, when followed, takes
you to the goal: freedom in that area. The most important front is presence,
control and internal speed. From control, all the rest are made possible.

This book intersperses all 11 fronts throughout the book, the same way Miracle Swimming classes are taught. You'll make a little progress here, then switch to another front and make a little progress there, then switch again and make some progress over there. Little by little, predictably and systematically, you grow. Growth happens quickly if you go slowly and skip no steps.

STEP 1: 2+2=4

If we know that 2+2=4, and we base our adding of 2+2 on this truth, we will get the correct answer every time. If we add 2+3, or 2+6, trying to get 4, we will never get the correct answer. Everything else based on the incorrect answer will be further afield of the truth.

That is why you should not expect to learn the freestyle (crawl stroke) or treading water, or how to breathe if your front float is tense, stiff and uncomfortable. A tense front float plus stroke mechanics do not equal a comfortable, in-control freestyle.

In learning to swim, the "correct answer" is comfort and control in water, not just the ability to go from here to there with tidy strokes. Once you have comfort and control, learning to go from here to there is automatic and guaranteed.

Historically, the formula of swimming instruction with students who are *not* afraid has been:

> A student who is not afraid
> + being taught only mechanics
>
> + being asked to keep up with the rest of the class
>
> + lack of discussion of how students feel
>
> + lack of instruction in how to remain in control
>
> > = a swimmer who is safe in most situations but has no idea what to do when he becomes afraid.

The commonly used formula for students who *are* afraid is:

> A student who is afraid
> + being taught only mechanics
>
> + being asked to keep up with the rest of the class
>
> + lack of discussion of how students feel or answers to their basic questions
>
> + lack of instruction in how to remain in control
>
>> = a person uncomfortable in water, "stroking" if he is lucky but not swimming. He is not safe, he is afraid in the deep, and he does not call himself a swimmer.

To get the correct answer, this sums it up:

> a student who is afraid or is not afraid
> + permission to learn at his own pace
>
> + an opportunity to share feelings and thoughts
>
> + learning how to stay in control
>
> + satisfactory answers to all his questions
>
> + all the learning steps of swimming in sequence
>
>> = a person who feels confident and safe, which allows him to access his natural ability, and without effort or thought, to make up the mechanics on the spot to go from here to there with ease, the same way a child learns to walk

It has been thought that by learning swimming mechanics—strokes—a student would overcome fear and gain control. However:

SWIMMING MECHANICS HAVE NO MEANING
UNTIL YOU CAN FEEL WHAT'S HAPPENING.

If you're terrified, you cannot feel what the water is doing for you.

13

> ## $2+2=4$
> MOST ADULTS LEARN TO SWIM TO ADD PEACE OF MIND AND PLEASURE TO THEIR LIVES. SINCE THE GOAL IS PEACE OF MIND AND PLEASURE IN WATER, PEACE OF MIND AND PLEASURE IN WATER ARE THE MOST IMPORTANT THINGS TO PRACTICE.

It's true that strokes give you control of something: direction, propulsion and speed. However, strokes don't make a person safe or confident. Millions of adults know how to do strokes, but are still afraid in deep pools and in open water. They're not in control in deep water, so how can they feel safe doing strokes? They don't. You must be in control in deep water in order to learn anything in deep water. The minimum level of control needed is control over yourself, not over direction, propulsion or speed. All afraid-in-water students I've met agree that they don't feel in control of themselves in deep water.

True or false:

YOU WANT YOUR SAFETY TO COME FROM YOURSELF, NOT FROM THE BOTTOM OR THE SIDE OF THE POOL.

By control, I don't mean that you're saying over and over to yourself, "I'm safe. Just do it. You can get there." Instead, I mean you can just be yourself in water, perfectly quiet within, and enjoy yourself without doing anything in particular. The water is so different from land that the experience of simply being in water or deep water is enough to be interesting, to arouse curiosity, to satisfy. Even if it weren't interesting, it would still be essential to be in control if you wanted to swim.

Being in water is bringing your full presence to it. It's being completely "there." Nothing is completely available to you and me unless we're experiencing it while we're completely there. In school when we were children, it was called "applying yourself." Only when we are completely "there" can we receive all that's being given and all that's inherently present. The gifts of being completely there can be "mind-blowing." In the case of learning how to be comfortable in the water—pool and ocean— my students have used that very term: mind blowing.

Have you ever "flown off the handle" and later regretted it? Surely we all have. Flying off the handle is loss of control in an irretrievable way. This is panic, the same as panic in deep water. The solution is the same for both, and it's simple. Naturally, this book is about the panic in water. The solution works for all panic.

When you're in control, you have choices. You can ask yourself, "Would I rather do this, or that?" When we're not in control, we act from a place of survival, habit, or automatic reactions that we can't change in the moment. It's almost as though we have no mind. Indeed, when we are in these moments, we have, for all intents and purposes, lost our minds.

$$2+2=4$$

WHEN YOU'RE NOT IN CONTROL, YOU DON'T HAVE CHOICE.

This book illustrates learning: the learning of you, a person, not just a physical body but a non-physical being who inhabits and controls the body. We use this essential truth of what you and I are to lead you to the steps of healing your fear and learning to swim. Healing fear and learning to swim are about what you do with your self, not your body. (Learning strokes is about what you do with your body, and that comes after learning to swim.) Without this fundamental point, you cannot efficiently learn to be in control and be confident in water. In fact, you have virtually no chance of becoming free in deep water.

2+2=4
IF YOU DON'T HAVE THE CORRECT INFORMATION, YOU HAVE LITTLE CHANCE OF SUCCESS.

Many people make it through swimming lessons without ever learning the essential non-physical skills of control. This is fine until an emergency in water comes up. And when emergencies come up, many swimmers don't know what to do. This is partly because they were never taught the fundamentals of safety. Most instructors believe fervently that they teach safety. But they were never trained in the fundamentals of safety themselves. (No one was, as far as I know.) Most adults in the United States (and the world?), even those who have taken swimming lessons, are not comfortable in deep open water and therefore they aren't safe: they could panic at any time. If control in water is taught, the results are more positive than students imagined possible. When we use this teaching at my swim school, students call their experience a miracle.

Please consider letting yourself off the hook for not having learned to swim yet. When you receive all the pertinent information (and learn it), you cannot possibly fail. Not that everyone has to overcome his or her fear with this method. But we have not seen any other teaching that gets to the heart of panic-prevention in water and remaining safe. The level of confidence you attain, the level of skill you attain and the degree of challenges you can meet are probably not optimal without this information.

> *"Focusing on comfort and overcoming fear is great. I needed to develop this level of comfort in the water before attempting to really try to swim."*
>
> -- Norbert

STEP 2: HOW TO STAY IN CONTROL

Where are you? Where is your self? If you were to point to yourself, where would you point? Go ahead: point to yourself now. Some people point to their heads. Some point to their hearts. What about you? If a surgeon opened you up there, would she find you? No, she wouldn't find *you*. She'd find bones and tissues but not you. You aren't physical. You have a physical body but you are non-physical.

We *have* bodies. We *have* feelings. We *have* thoughts. Who is it that has these things? You and I, each a spirit, have them. We are spirit, first.

Do you agree that we humans are spiritual beings living in physical bodies in a physical world? It's useful to think of ourselves as spirit, or as energy. When we think of ourselves as formless energy, or spirit, it gives us a new understanding of our freedom of "movement." I don't mean freedom of physical movement. We already understand that we're free to move our limbs, if we are able-bodied. I'm referring to your movement as spirit in a body. In other words, how do you move while your body is still?

Your body conforms to physical laws like the laws of gravity. Your spirit, however, doesn't conform to physical laws. It is not physical. This must be taken into account in order for teaching (and learning) to be most effective.

You are the one who controls your body. You are the one that instructors must communicate with, the one whose trust they must earn and whose attention they must keep. You must be in control of your self and your body in water. Otherwise teaching won't work and learning won't happen.

To get to the bottom of learning, we must understand and address both the non-physical you—which I call you, your self, or spirit—and the body.

> ## 2+2=4
> ONCE YOU'RE IN CONTROL OF YOURSELF, YOU CAN THEN BE IN CONTROL OF YOUR BODY.

When you start a swimming class, you may wonder, "How can I stand to put my face in water? How can I remain safe in deep water?" Good questions. These must be answered before anyone can expect you to "hear" anything else about swimming.

When using this book, please remain safe and in control in the water by *doing only what you want to do*. While learning to overcome fear, *never put yourself into a position where you have to do something you don't like, or don't want to do.*

It's important to do only that which you want to do because that's the only way we can be sure that you will be present for it. If you do something you don't really want to do, part of you resists what the other part of you is doing. That means you're divided against yourself. You're not fully "there."

If you aren't fully there, how can you expect yourself to learn? How can anyone else expect you to learn?

> ## 2+2=4
> YOU MUST BE PRESENT TO LEARN.

You need to enjoy yourself. Don't you owe that to yourself? Being present and having fun are two things that swimming lessons have never required. Students who are afraid are often thinking, "Will the instructor ask me to do something I don't want to do? Will I drown? Am I safe? What if I panic? How will I get air? How will I stand up? Will I make a fool of myself? What if I sink?"

2+2=4

YOU CAN'T LEARN WHAT TO DO WITH YOUR ARMS AND LEGS IF YOU'RE AFRAID YOU MIGHT NOT LIVE.

What do I mean by being present? I mean that you know where you are, you know what you're doing, and you're in control. You're satisfied with how you're handling things. Everyone can learn to swim if they practice the right things. And, it's fun...so my students have told me for over 20 years.

2+2=4

TO REMAIN IN CONTROL OF YOURSELF, YOU MUST KEEP YOURSELF AS A SPIRIT IN YOUR BODY.

Take a moment to absorb what this means.

If you have taken swimming lessons before and you've worried about your safety, it was impossible to be successful learning mechanics. By learning, I mean that you embodied the mechanics so that you could perform them anytime without thinking.

Here is a diagram of being present:

Present: You and your body are in the same place. The stick figure represents your body. The circle and the space within it represent you, spirit. In this situation you'd say, "I feel good."

When you're present, your spirit and your body are in the same space. In the graphic above, the circle and the area within it represent your presence. They represent you as a spirit: your self. In the diagram, you and your body are together. You're "there." You're in control of your body. You feel safe. You're as calm and comfortable as if you were reading the Sunday paper on the couch. You could be taking a walk. You're at ease. In our everyday language, we call this being present, "at home," composed, grounded, centered, together. You feel poised, quiet, solid, in control, stable, peaceful, balanced, open, comfortable.

Here's a diagram of nervousness: beginning to lose presence. It can happen on land, in the water, or anywhere:

Nervous:

You'd say, "I feel nervous, but I'm okay."

We call this situation "nervous." You don't feel terrible, but you don't feel good anymore, as you did in the first circle. You're mostly in control, but not completely. In everyday language, we call this, "having cold feet." "A question in the air." "Buzzing." As a spirit, you aren't completely in the body anymore. You've begun to rise upward and outward through the top of your head.

Here's a diagram of when you've become still more afraid

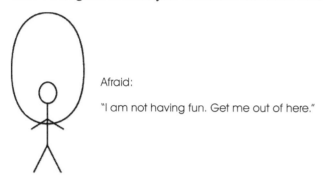

Afraid:

"I am not having fun. Get me out of here."

Afraid: you are further out of your body. There's little or no presence of you as a spirit in your body below the chest. This causes the common knot in the stomach, butterflies in the stomach, and clammy hands and feet. In the diagram the hands are drawn below the circle so that you can see this. There's less presence of the spirit in the body to keep things stable. We're no longer having fun when we reach this stage.

Here's a diagram of us when we're terrified:

Paralyzed by fear:

"Help!"

Your spirit has left your body all the way to your neck. There's no presence of you below the neck. You can't move a muscle. We call this "scared stiff" or "paralyzed by fear." If we're out of the body a little bit further, above the mouth, we're unable to call for help; we can't make a sound or even mouthe a word.

Finally, here's a diagram of panic:

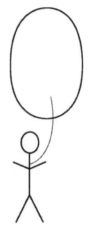

Panic: Out of it. "How do I get back? I can't get back."

We call this "losing it;" gone; panic; not home; out of it; freaked out. "Out" is quite correct. The spirit is out of the body, not permanently, and not completely, but enough for the body to be in danger. There's still a thin thread of energy that connects us to our bodies when we are in panic. If we return to the body, it's not because we're in control of doing so: it just happens.

If, once you return from panic, someone asked you what happened, you would say you don't know. This is because you weren't there to experience it. You left your body first. Someone watching you could tell you what you did (what your body did), but you wouldn't remember since you weren't "there."

WHAT IS CONTROL?

It's purposely or automatically keeping yourself, as a spirit, completely in your body.

PANIC PREVENTION

2+2=4
TO OVERCOME YOUR FEAR IN WATER YOU NEED TO KNOW HOW TO REMAIN IN CONTROL AND PREVENT PANIC.

Remaining in control is the key to the door of confidence. It begins with the awareness that you have a choice to stay "here" or leave. The next step is *choosing* to stay here or leave (to give up). Once you decide to stay here, the next step is to *feel*. Feeling keeps you here, in your body. The next step is to follow the instructions that come to you. All of this takes place in a couple of seconds.

If we have no choice when certain situations arise, that is if panic is a habit, then there's no chance to remain in control on purpose. We're in the throes of our habit. Only when we slow down can we have a choice. Without slowing down, there is no learning of panic prevention.

Question: Slow down what?
Answer: Slow down our internal speed: our vibration. You and I have various internal "speeds." When we're calm, our speed is very slow, or still. When we're not calm, our energy moves faster. Our incremental speeds can be called calm, contentedness, interest, fascination, concern, watchfulness, protectiveness, nervousness, fear and struggling and panic. No doubt, we've all felt these increments of internal speed. When we're struggling, our energy is moving—vibrating—very fast.

Q: How do I slow down my internal speed, my vibration?
A: By *feeling it and allowing it to be there*.

Q: How can this be fun?
A: By taking it slowly, only doing what's comfortable and taking plenty of rests. The process really is rewarding. It heals fear.

Once we slow things down enough, we have a choice. From the choice not to panic we can then exercise the steps to keep ourselves in control. From exercising these steps, we maintain the highest degree of safety that's possible in the moment.

23

Your Vibration or Internal Speed

We may think of ourselves as having no input over how fast our internal "speed" is. We may suddenly find ourselves "speeding" and feel stuck there. We are "rattled."

When you feel tension, you are speeding to some degree. You can learn what to do with this speed.

Location, Location, Location

The five circle diagrams are the main stages we go through when we're in a situation and we become more afraid. However, just because they're typical stages, it doesn't mean they're desirable or required. In fact, they're not helpful. It would be preferable if we could stay in the first circle even when something very frightening is happening.

If you're chopping vegetables in the kitchen and you cut your finger while thinking about your children driving home in a blizzard, where are you? Are you completely in the kitchen? No. Part of you is in the kitchen and part of you is in the car. You wouldn't say to yourself, "Here's my knife, here's my finger, I'll slice right here." You were not in complete control of your hands or the knife. You could not control your body (hands) since you weren't in it.

Where You Are Relative to Your Body

You and I enter, leave, and remain in our bodies at different times of the day. When we're "at home," we're in our bodies, calm and relaxed. We're in our bodies when we feel in control.

If you're sitting at your desk at work daydreaming about being in Hawaii, your body is at your desk but you are in Hawaii. If someone knocks on your door, the sound brings you back to your desk. If you're reading a book and you have to read the same paragraph three times, your body is in the chair but you are somewhere else.

We can be "at home," solidly in our bodies. We can be partly in and partly out, and cut our finger with a knife. And, we can be completely out—when we panic and can't stop ourselves.

Likewise, when we're focused on something that's not happening now, in a fantasy of the future (what will happen if...?) or a memory of the past (I can't let X happen again), *we are in* the future or in the past. We are not here. If you're in the water and you're not completely here, you're not in control. Don't even think about *learning to swim* in this situation. This is when you can easily fly out to the third, fourth or fifth circles, even if there's no physical danger.

The farther out you go past the first circle, the easier it is to go out even farther. We humans have formed a habit of letting ourselves jump out of the present into the future to "protect ourselves from danger." Sometimes, it's necessary to protect ourselves. At other times, it's not appropriate because there's no danger or because we'd be better off staying here and attending to what our bodies are telling us. They tell us how to be safe...as safe as we can be.

In the not-dangerous times it's *useful* to keep ourselves in the present: in control. In the dangerous times it's *essential* to keep ourselves in our bodies. Otherwise we are of no use to our bodies. This may be why you are afraid in water.

Because the fundamental act of remaining in control is about *where you are* relative to your body, we can say that being in control is a matter of your location. In your body, you're in control. When you're partly, or completely out of your body, you're partly, or completely out of control.

Since the fundamental act of remaining safe is about your location as a spirit relative to your body, learning is a spirit-ual event. Obviously this has nothing to do with religion. It's about the location and movement of you as spirit.

For learning to be optimal, we must take into account our characteristics as spirit. The fact that we are spiritual beings is so ordinary and invisible that it has been overlooked in most teaching. Overcoming fear and learning to swim are spiritual and physical events. First and foremost, especially for people who are afraid, overcoming fear is spiritual.

Q: How Long Does It Take to Go From the First Circle to the Fifth?

Going from calm to panic: leaving your body. © M. Dash 1983

A: No time flat. You can be feeling fine one moment and in the next moment, panic. You've probably experienced this.

Q: Who's in Charge of Which Circle You're In?

A: Right. *You* are. You may think that *circumstances* caused you to leave your body and go to the next circle. But circumstances were not the cause. A belief you had at the time was the cause (for example, "I will sink. I'm not safe. I will drown.") This belief caused you to leave the first circle. If you knew *why you must stay* in your body, you'd think twice about leaving. But you didn't know the importance of your location.

$2+2=4$

IF YOU DON'T KNOW YOU'RE IN CONTROL
OF YOUR LOCATION, YOU AREN'T

Once we know that moving out of the first circle is what causes us to lose control, we can learn how to remain in the first circle and in control on purpose. This is simple.

Why Would Anyone Leave the First Circle if Doing So Would Put Him in Danger?

Please don't blame yourself: it's a learned response. We learn when we're children to leave the first circle. We leave our bodies when we would rather not feel what's happening. Fear, emotional and physical pain or any situation you can think of that would be too much to bear is reason enough to leave. A 5 year old being held under water by his playful older brother past the point of fun or safety can either stay in his body and feel extreme discomfort (no air, desperation, possibly rage) or he can leave his body. Who would stay? No one.

Leaving the first circle becomes an adaptation to great pain. Over time, it can become a habit. When it appears that something is going to feel bad, or we're reminded of something that felt bad, we leave our bodies. No one can be blamed for it. We began doing it long before we knew the consequences: losing control. But this habit can be replaced with a more useful one: the habit of staying here. This is the path to freedom in water.

In this book we will learn first how to be safe and be in control: how to stay in the first circle and return to it if you notice you're in the second. We don't go to a higher circle than that. We prevent it. You can be in control enough to prevent it.

When you *know* you're safe, you exert no effort or thought to remain in the first circle. When you're *not sure* you're safe, you need to know how to remain in the first circle, or how to get back to it, on purpose.

BEING IN CONTROL

> "If I know that I can't put my feet on the bottom, I panic."
> "I can fake it for a while, but then the truth comes and gets me."
> —Sylvia

If you ever learned to drive or ride a bike, ski or in-line skate, you know you didn't feel safe until you learned how to stop. It's the same in swimming. You need to know how to stop in order to feel safe. Stop your arms and legs? No, stop yourself from panicking. Once you can remain stopped, you can learn the simple building blocks and mechanics of swimming.

> CONTROL GIVES CONFIDENCE
> CONFIDENCE FEEDS LEARNING

Overcoming fear *must* precede learning to swim. Otherwise, the feelings of ease and freedom you desire to play, rest, and swim in shallow and deep water are not possible.

It's more important to stay in the first circle than to float or to put your face in the water, to stand up, or to tread water. If you stay in the first circle, you'll be in control of whether you inhale water or not, stand up or stay floating, stay speedy or slow down. Once you can remain in control, you can do whatever you want to do. Do you see the importance of being in the first circle?

2+2=4

YOU MUST BE ABLE TO REMAIN IN THE FIRST CIRCLE
IN ORDER TO LEARN TO SWIM, BREATHE WHILE
SWIMMING, AND REST IN DEEP WATER.

How to Stay in Control

You can stay in control (in the first circle) by *feeling. Everything.* That's right. Slow down and *feel* everything that's happening in the moment. Feel whatever is there. Feel your internal "speed," feel buoyancy, feel tension, feel your chair, feel the air temperature, feel how much air you have or don't have, feel your left knee. Just feel. If feeling all of that is too much, just feel one of them. You'll probably have to slow down to feel.

DON'T EVEN THINK ABOUT SKIPPING THE STEP OF FEELING

To be in control, we have to feel. And because feeling happens in only one place—our bodies—when we focus on what we're feeling, we stay in our bodies. Where our focus is, we are. Feeling keeps us in our bodies and keeps us in control.

Often, we use thinking to negotiate an unfamiliar situation. But in some situations, such as overcoming your fear in water, thinking does not work best. It works better to feel. When we think too much, we lose touch with feelings.

If you let yourself feel, you'll get a sense of what to do next. Proceed slowly enough to keep feeling. Follow your internal "instructions." Give yourself permission (and get permission from anyone you're with) to slow down and feel. You need to stay slow. If you do this, you cannot help but succeed.

Please let yourself off the hook for not learning to swim if you tried before. You were probably not asked to go slowly and listen to your internal signals, feel them, and follow their instructions. These were absolutely essential!

Have you watched a baby learn to walk? She didn't hurry herself. She didn't try to run before she could walk. She didn't criticize herself while she learned. She didn't compete with the neighbor baby or compare herself with other toddlers at daycare. She was completely self-absorbed, that is, 100% in her body. She was in the first circle. That's why a skill as intricate as walking only takes a few weeks for a baby to learn completely.

STEP 3: PERMISSION TO GO AT YOUR OWN PACE

Where you are right now with your swimming is precisely the perfect place for you. Without effort, you'll find your way to your goals and your goals will find their way to you. Gradually, as you spend time in the water and you open to new thoughts and feelings, you move forward. Change happens, sometimes in the pool, sometimes between pool sessions, sometimes in your dreams.

You may have a sense of new information coming to you. Simply by picking up this book, something began to shift. An opening was created. Each conscious and unconscious moment that you're engaged in this book you'll fill in a bit of space in this new opening. Trust that you're doing exactly what's appropriate for you just by being yourself. You'll reach your swimming goals simply by doing what's fun.

Let yourself move one easy step at a time. Be there for each step. Experience the water. Listen to your body: it will tell you what you need to know in the moment. When you're "home," i.e., in your body, you can hear what it tells you. You automatically translate that into security, action, floating, swimming. However if you're not home, you can't hear your body's instructions or take care of yourself well. When the time comes, if you're practicing a skill that doesn't seem to be working, stop and come back to your body. Better yet, don't practice a physical skill: practice only being in your body. Out of this, a physical skill will arise.

Only your body can tell you when it's time to do something new. You learn beautifully when you go at your own pace. In fact, nothing can prevent you from progressing all the way to your goals if you go at your own pace.

> *Your method has allowed me to go as slowly as I want, which I've never experienced before in learning a new sport. I'm really excited about swimming, being in water for the first time in my life, and welcoming the whole new world that is opening up to me.*
> —Darlene

STEP 4: WHAT IS SAFETY?

As mentioned above, for the purposes of this course, safety is your ability to remain in control of yourself. Safety is also having choices about how to respond, rather than responding automatically but inappropriately, due to panic.

Yes, there's another kind of safety too...the pool rules: "don't run on the deck, don't push, don't chew gum in the pool (to avoid choking), don't leave your child unattended at the pool." But your ability to remain in control of yourself in water is the key to enjoying every day at the pool, making intelligent choices and coming through a common swimming misadventure unharmed.

What's a misadventure? It's accidentally bumping into someone in the water, or getting a nose full of water or stepping into a hole at the lake. These things happen. Handling these events easily with no concern whatsoever is about remaining present.

Handling surprises well

Being in your body

2+2=4

IF A PERSON REMAINS IN CONTROL, HE HAS A BETTER CHANCE OF REMAINING SAFE THAN IF HE LOSES CONTROL

For example, if someone loses control, he may inhale while he's still under water. Or, he may thrash in just 3 feet of water, keeping himself below the surface instead of simply standing up. In both these situations, the person is "not there." He is out of his body. If he were present, he wouldn't do these things.

As we've said, the solution was always thought to be, "learn to swim." The solution is, actually, "learn to stay present."

If you were present, you'd be able to feel the water holding you up. You'd be able to feel that you still have enough air to stand up or get to the side. You'd be able to see how close to the surface you are or that you're at the surface already. If you weren't at the surface, you'd be able to take yourself there and get air even if you had never learned how to do it before. If you were present, you'd be "notified" by your intuition what your next step is—guaranteed. When you need to know something and you're calm, your next step just comes to you. Have you found this to be true in other parts of your life? *This is how you learned to walk.*

How to Stay in Your Body.

Feel. Go slowly. If you focus on your feeling, whatever the feeling is, whether ease or tension, warm or cold, happy or sad, your focus will be in your body. Since you can't be in two places at once, if you feel, you'll keep yourself in your body. You'll prevent yourself from panicking. You will be in the very place that healing takes place. *Herein lies one of the most powerful skills we can perform as humans: remaining in control— remaining in our bodies.* If you follow this book, you'll learn to prevent panic and stay in control. You'll learn it by overcoming your fear in water. The message is repeated often to help you develop this new habit in the water.

Is It Easy to Remain Present?

Let's go back to the diagram of the five circles of the spirit leaving the body.

Losing control: leaving your body © M. Dash 1983

33

Review:

Q: Why would we leave our bodies, if this causes us to lose control?

A: We leave because we don't want to feel pain, physical or emotional.

But, we're not *in control of* avoiding the pain. We avoid it by habit:

Approaching pain → LEAVE
Approaching pain → LEAVE

Breaking this habit is a step toward more empowered living, and freedom in water. *Slow down and feel.* If you slow down early enough, pain (in the form of anxiety) will not be a factor. If you practice this in the pool, keeping yourself in your body will become a habit.

In extreme situations, it might be essential to call heavily on this new muscle, the muscle of being able to keep yourself in your body to remain in control. Hopefully you'll never be in such a situation. But if you are, it can save your life.

To make it comfortable to stay present if you begin to feel afraid, slow down or stop. Feel just a "teaspoon" at a time. Go at your own pace. Leaving your body (panicking) would be worse.

STEP 5: GOING SLOWLY

Make it easy for yourself to remain in control.

You don't have to jump into the deep end on your first day. If you start slowly and do whatever allows you to remain in control at all times, you'll overcome your fear. You'll come to situations that used to make you afraid and you'll be able to handle them with new ease. For now, take them very slowly. You may have to stay in one place for a while. This is the natural process of healing and learning. Go slowly enough that you don't mind feeling your feelings. Sometimes it requires time, writing, talking, and feeling things you hadn't planned to feel. Give thanks. It's part of the process of becoming more yourself and free in water. The process looks different for each person and each person's process is right.

Fun Learning

STEP 6: STAY TRUE TO YOURSELF

It can be said that the "first circle" is a picture of what it looks like to stay true to yourself. In the first circle, you and your body are in the same place: you're "true."

Being "in true" is a term used about bicycle wheels and spokes when they are in perfect alignment. Stay in true, yourself.

Staying true to yourself
Being in your body

Each time you make a decision that allows you to stay true to yourself, you build self-trust. You build a foundation—an energy grid—an infrastructure of confidence within you.

Light infrastructure

Relatively few choices made to stay true to yourself. Relatively little confidence.

Much greater infrastructure

Many choices made to stay true to yourself. Relatively high confidence.

If you want to do X, do it. If you don't want to do X, don't do it. If not doing X makes you feel worse, then you actually do want to do it. Doing it will build self-trust.

If, in the water, you're curious about something and you feel safe exploring it, stay true to yourself and explore it. Not doing so could be disappointing.

If you want to explore something in the water and y
to stay true to yourself—to stay in the first circle
for help or make it feel safe in another way.

> ## $2+2=4$
> WHATEVER IT TAKES FOR YOU TO STAY
> TRUE TO YOURSELF IS WORTH DOING

Learning will happen if you stay true to yourself. If you don't, you'll delay
or prevent learning.

STEP 7: HAVE FUN

Where you are when you're having fun

TWO KINDS OF FUN

What are your beliefs about having fun in water? Do you believe you can
have fun doing things in any part of the pool? Is this too hard to believe?

Learning can be fun, as you surely know. You may still wonder if it can be
fun to learn to swim. This book is written to make each step small enough
that nothing is scary, you understand everything you're doing, and you're
game for each new experience. People tell me that each new experience is
fun. If it's *not* fun, stop. Find another way. Ask yourself what you would
enjoy doing that's in between where you are and where you want to be.
Tiny steps are safest for keeping things fun.

37

fun is a most natural state for you. A willingness to go slowly
stay comfortable will pave your way to a good experience. Are you
lling to take the time?

$$2 + 2 = 4$$

DO WHAT'S FUN

There are two kinds of fun. We often think of fun as the way we feel when
we're doubled over, slapping our knees laughing. That's one kind of fun.

In the other kind of fun you're not necessarily doubled over laughing, but if
someone were to ask you if you wanted to stop, you'd say no. You're having
a different kind of fun: exploring, satisfying your curiosity, absorbing
information, finding a new path, doing something you want to do.

Everything in this book—every step—is designed to be fun. We learn so
naturally and easily when we have fun. We don't use effort, yet we learn
anyway.

If something stops being fun as you practice the teachings of this book,
stop. Change the subject. Being unhappy is not a good use of your time.
It's not worthwhile…unless you're having fun being unhappy. (Don't
laugh. I've seen it, and you probably have, too.)

IF IT'S NOT FUN, DON'T DO IT

You may say, "Sometimes if I push myself I have a breakthrough." Outside
the pool, this is common. If you pulled all-nighters as a student in order
to turn in a paper in the morning, pushing helped. If you're an athlete and
you push yourself during competition in order to do better, pushing makes
a difference. In the pool, if it's *fun* to push, go ahead. If it's not fun, *stop*.

2+2=4

IF YOU'RE NOT HAVING FUN, YOU'RE NOT IN THE FIRST CIRCLE. IT'S NECESSARY TO HAVE FUN.

When you're overcoming fear, any "breakthroughs" that are accomplished by pushing will not stick. Pushing yourself to perform a skill so that you can check it off your list is an empty victory. Further, it's not stable. Many swimming students have been told by their instructors, "There! You've got it. Now you just need to practice." But the students knew in their bones that they didn't have it, even if it looked as if they did.

The most important reason to avoid pushing is that it's scary: it takes you out of the first circle. We have established (well, I have…have you?) that it's our #1 priority to practice being in the first circle all the time: practice comfort and control to become expert at comfort and control. You don't need to be better at scaring yourself. So don't practice anything that puts you in the second or higher circle.

If you feel even a hint of frustration, back up, regroup and start again. Regrouping looks like this:

It fell apart.

I regrouped.

39

If there's another hint of frustration, *stop* and change the subject to a different front. You don't have to have a crummy time learning to swim. It can all be fun. If it's not one kind of fun or the other, you're pushing. Come back to the first circle where you can enjoy yourself.

> ## PUSHING HINDERS LEARNING

STEP 8: YOUR GOALS AND WILDEST DREAMS

Identifying your goals and wildest dreams for swimming expands your thinking. Write down your goals for learning to swim:

1. _____
2. _____
3. _____
4. _____

Is comfort your Number 1 goal? I hope so, but I'm not allowed to vote. Now write down your wildest dreams for swimming. Be outrageous. No holds barred!

1. _____
2. _____
3. _____
4. _____

When you identify and write down your goals, you establish a direction for yourself. It's more powerful to state them in words, spoken or written, than to simply think about them. By writing down your goals and wildest dreams, you add weight to them. You anchor them in your infrastructure. If you tell someone your goals, someone you trust, you anchor them still deeper.

If you were to show someone where your goals were relative to your arms' reach, where would they be?

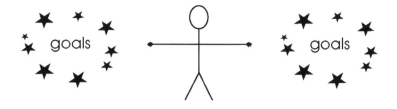

Your goals are just outside your present reach.
It requires stretching or growth to reach them.

They would probably be just beyond your present reach. Accomplishing them requires stretching or growth.

Now, relative to your arms' reach, where would your wildest dreams be?

Wildest
Dreams
Next Town

Your wildest dreams are well beyond your present reach but since they reach further, *you* reach further. You grow. This wide expanse is your mental space "assigned" to reaching your swimming dreams. You may have heard the phrase, "space abhors a vacuum." The larger the empty space, the more information you'll naturally pull in to fill it. This requires no effort.

STEP 9: YOUR RELATIONSHIP TO YOUR GOALS

Here you sit, in your chair. Nearby are the goals you want to reach. What's between you and your goals? How do you feel about them? Will you need to conquer them? Cajole them? Chase them? Trick them? Work hard? Push yourself? Grow?

Would it work to be graceful with them? To give them room?

Often we think of our goals, especially if they've been elusive, as something we have to bear down upon and work hard to reach. We brace ourselves for the big push.

If you feel this way about your swimming goals, will it help you get started? Not likely.

Between you and your goals are your feelings about them—and also the steps required to reach them. Let's talk about feelings for a moment.

If there were a new person with whom you wanted to have dinner and you did all the work of arranging the details—calling him/her, making reservations at a restaurant and time of his/her choice, picking him/her up, taking him/her home—and you continued to try to build a friendship by handling all the details yourself date after date, would the relationship work? Probably not. Many of us have tried it.

It's the same with your relationship to your goals. Your part of the relationship is to do what's fun and comfortable—what you feel good about. The rest is out of your hands.

At times you may be afraid that you won't reach the goal. You may think you're doing something wrong, and try to figure it out. This causes you to go into your head and disconnect from your body's knowing and the hope and the optimism you started with. The truth is, nothing's wrong: it's inevitable that you'll reach your swimming goal if you're willing to do what's fun and let it come at its own pace.

What if you treated your goals with respect? Gave them room? Didn't crowd them, chase them or threaten them? When you insist that they hurry, they retreat. When you're willing to give them all the time they need and you enjoy the ride, they come as soon as possible.

You may say again, "But many times I reach my goals by pushing." True. And there are times when pushing is appropriate. The process of learning to overcome fear, however, is not one of those times. Try *not* pushing yourself and see how it works. You'll find that not only is it healing, but you'll enjoy yourself in water perhaps for the first time. You'll build a new you in the water. You'll get there just by trusting your intuition.

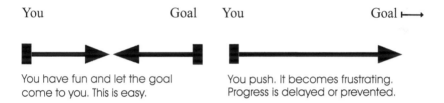

You   Goal   You   Goal ⟼

You have fun and let the goal   You push. It becomes frustrating.
come to you. This is easy.   Progress is delayed or prevented.

STEP 10: RECOGNIZE THE FULL IMPACT ON YOUR LIFE OF BEING AFRAID IN WATER...AND ITS BENEFITS

List the ways that your life has been impacted by being afraid in water:

1. _____
2. _____
3. _____
4. _____
5. _____
6. _____

Now answer this question: How has my fear in water served me in my life? What has been *good* about it?

Sometimes people think this is a trick question. It's not meant to be. There are *benefits* you have derived (fairly, innocently) from being afraid in water. How has it come in handy for you? List the ways here:

1. _____

2. _____

3. _____

To help you remember the benefits, note some that other people have listed:

_____ I didn't have to worry about being seen in a bathing suit.

_____ It allowed me to stay safe rather than taking risks.

_____ I didn't have to worry about ruining my hair.

_____ I didn't have to be vulnerable or look as though I didn't know what I was doing.

_____ I didn't have to worry about my makeup.

_____ I received attention from my family and friends.

_____ I had more time for myself.

_____ It brought me closer to another family member who also couldn't swim.

_____ It allowed me to become closer to a group of people for whom it was "hip" to not swim.

_____ It kept me alive because I stayed away from dangerous situations.

_____ I have a great story about why I don't swim.

_____ I saved money on bathing suits since mine never wore out.

_____ I got many father/family points for playing with the kids instead of going to a swimming social function.

_____ There were no benefits whatsoever. I was always missing the fun. I was embarrassed that I couldn't participate.

Be as honest as you can be with yourself. If there's something you don't accept in yourself, sometimes it's more difficult to be honest about it. You can only be as honest as you are self-accepting.

Honesty gets you to your goal most quickly. You're the only person who sees your answers. Your answers are okay, whatever they are. As an instructor of this teaching, I believe I have heard *everything* and I never heard a response that was not understandable. It's okay to have the beliefs you have even if they sound silly to you.

Now that you've begun a process of overcoming your fear, you've indirectly said, "By undertaking this learning, I am giving up the benefits I once derived from being afraid in water." Ask yourself, "Am I ready to be finished with these benefits?" If you're ready to be finished with them, fine.

If not, that's fine, too. It's helpful just to know the truth. If you're not finished with one or more of them, it's completely okay. Don't push yourself to be done with them. Let yourself be where you are. In some way they make you feel safe. They are healing you.

By identifying the benefits of being afraid in water, you have now given yourself a choice. Having a choice is a great place to be.

> ## HAVING A CHOICE MEANS YOU'RE IN CONTROL.

It doesn't matter *what* you choose: it just matters that you have a choice. Make a choice to accept the benefits you derive from being afraid and let them be there. They are okay. Make a choice to accept yourself just as you are. Or, make a choice to give up the benefits because you're finished with them. *One choice is not better or more advanced than the other.* The goal is to be true to yourself. If you cannot accept that you're where you are with regard to your beliefs, perhaps you can accept that you cannot accept it. *That's good enough.*

STEP 11: UNDERSTANDING SELF-CONSCIOUSNESS

If you anticipate that you might feel self-conscious at the pool, ask yourself where "you" are. You're over in someone else's eyes looking back at yourself. That's a good example of being out of your body. If you come back "home," you can do what's best for you.

Chances are that if someone's watching you they're *interested* in what you're doing, not being critical. Then they lose interest. There's a chance that they're on the deck because they cannot yet do what you're learning to do. Why are most of the adults on the deck, in chairs? Maybe they don't want to get wet, or maybe they're afraid. Why are adults in the water bobbing around in the shallow end, not swimming? Could some of them be afraid, too?

If you feel self-conscious, remember this: you're there for yourself only, and only you can give this to yourself. You have your best chance of success if you keep your focus on yourself and honor the *feeling in your body*. This is practicing staying in your body. And this practice will take you where you want to go in swimming.

STEP 12: WARM UP TO GETTING IN

You may now be ready to think about getting into the water. If you understand what I've said so far, we're on the same page. Are you ready to find a pool? To get into it? What do you feel when you think about it? Excitement? Fear? Nervousness? If it doesn't feel like fun to think about it, then what would make it fun? Going with a friend? Not pushing yourself? Being in a class? Being near a lifeguard? Being warm? Being in a pool with no deep end? Having no splashing kids around? Not going at all? All of these are okay.

One reason for using warm pools is that fear, itself, is cold. Generally someone who is afraid in water is colder in the pool than someone who is not afraid.

> ### Why Pools (and You) Should Be Warm for Learning
>
> An ideal water temperature for learning is 93° to 95° F. That's hot for air, but not for water. Warmth makes all the difference in your ability to enjoy yourself and stay present.
>
> You'll probably be most comfortable in a pool that is 93° or so. When you're warm, you can focus on your practice. In school, would you have been expected to learn in classrooms that were 40 degrees? Likewise, learning pools should be warm. In the early stages of learning, there's not a lot of activity. You need to be warm without exercising. In our classes we are in the water for two hours at a time. This allows us to relax and go slowly. Students are very happy with the warm pool temperatures and the time we have in the water.
>
> If you can't find a warm pool, I suggest purchasing a 1.5-millimeter wetsuit (neoprene) shirt. A thin wetsuit like this should do the trick. It adds a bit of buoyancy but it won't hurt your learning at all. The wetsuit is tremendously worthwhile. And who knows? Little wetsuits shirts could become trendy.
>
> When trying on and purchasing a wetuit shirt, make sure it has zero gaps and zero wrinkles. It should be *very* snug.

Step 13: Set Yourself Up to Succeed

Create the situation you need in order to be comfortable. What would a fun, successful visit to the pool be like? Set up your visit so that you can enjoy yourself. Write it here:

1. _____

2. _____

3. _____

Try not to compromise. To compromise in this case may not be staying true to yourself. Go to this pool. Observe the setting. What's going on? Will you be able to feel in control there if you follow your plan?

FINDING THE RIGHT POOL

To maximize your chances of success, look for the right pool. Ideally it will be:

1. warm (93° to 95° F, 35° C)

2. in a convenient location

3. available at hours that work for you

4. clean.

For a list of pools in your area, if you're online, go to www.swimmersguide.com. Most heated swimming pools are kept at temperatures between 80° and 84°. Some are kept between 85° and 90°. Pools in the 80's feel chilly to most new swimmers. Typically you can find warm pools at centers for people with disabilities, at an Easter Seals organization, or a hospital therapy pool. There are also warm pools in hot springs locations (this is where we teach some of our classes). Some of the cities where there are centers for people with disabilities are San Francisco (the Janet Pomeroy Center), Minneapolis (the Courage Center), and Albany, New York. Some hotels have warm pools and allow community swimming. Call around.

At centers for people with disabilities, you may need a prescription to use the pool, as this is how their insurance coverage is structured. These prescriptions can be acquired from a doctor or health care practitioner. If you're self-conscious about asking for this prescription, take note: are you outside of your body? If so, bring yourself back and do what's best for you.

STEP 14: STARTING FROM CALM

When you're learning something new, you'll be most in control if you let yourself be where you are.

If you're not calm, stop and feel your discomfort. Don't try to make it disappear. Bring your attention, your self, all the way into your body. What does your body need in order to be comfortable? Give it to yourself, whatever it is. Don't proceed until you're comfortable.

It doesn't matter *what* you do to be calm. It only matters that you feel calm and in control. This can't be emphasized enough. You can enjoy yourself. That's the whole point. If you're enjoying yourself, you'll want to continue.

Your new awareness and familiarity with water automatically emerge when you're in your body, listening to your body and letting yourself feel. Give yourself time to come home. From here, new ideas and information come to you.

Simply by being committed to your swimming and following the steps in this book—or even reading them—you've accelerated the learning/healing process.

STEP 15: BEING IN YOUR BODY VS. BEING IN YOUR HEAD

Here is an exercise that someone could read slowly to you as you listen. One student read it into her answering machine and then played it back:

Close your eyes. Think about your breakfast this morning. Did you have breakfast? Did you have your favorite breakfast? Did you go out for breakfast? Did you eat alone?

Now feel your feet. Feel your feet inside your shoes. Feel their temperature. Are they warm enough? Are they comfortable? Do they feel squeezed?

Now think about breakfast again. What did you have? Did you read as you ate? Were you in a hurry? Did you relax?

Now feel your feet again. What position are they in? Are they moving? How are your toes? Now think about breakfast again. Did you have enough to eat?

Notice how your location changes as you go from breakfast to your feet. When you think about breakfast, where do you experience your attention to be? In your head? Behind or above your head? When you're thinking of breakfast, do you have any sensations in your feet?

When you feel your feet, what is your location? Notice that you move down from your head. Notice that you *feel* your feet and bring an awareness to them that was not there when you were thinking about breakfast.

It's useful to know how *feeling* changes the location of your awareness: the location of you. By being aware of how you feel, you tune into your body and yourself.

Today or soon, go back to this place you've found to go swimming and get into the water. Take the easy route. Here's a diagram of you on the easy route. Once you're in the water, just stand there. Absorb the surroundings. Hold onto the wall. Lean against it and breathe. You're in the water. You're on a new path.

Stay as long as you're enjoying yourself. There's nothing else to do for now.

More fun learning

CONTRACT WITH YOURSELF

I, _____ , have decided once and for all that I want to overcome my fear of being in water (shallow or deep) and to learn to swim the way I've always dreamt I could. I agree to give myself the best possible chance of learning. This means I will (check all that you agree to):

____ give myself all the time it takes

____ allow myself to stay safe all the time

____ allow myself to have fun all the time

____ stay comfortable

____ learn what it feels like to stay in my body

____ learn how to bring myself back into my body

____ allow myself to leave the pool while I am still happy

____ check my beliefs from time to time to measure my progress

____ be honest with myself

____ be gentle with myself

____ examine, if the opportunity arises, any lack of gentleness, and review the section about it in this book (Steps 51 and 53)

____ know that if I do these things, I can only succeed in reaching my goals.

Signed, _____

Date _____

Any lingering thoughts? List them here:

1. _____

2. _____

STEP 16: GET THE BIG PICTURE

When you decide to learn to swim and then you do something about it, you have a natural propensity to pay attention, follow directions, and try to do things correctly so that the instructions will work. You want to "get it" and you're prepared to work for it.

Rest easy. You'll get it. It's not that you'll get it if you do everything "perfectly." It's not that you'll get it if you push yourself. It's simply that when you let yourself have fun and proceed at a comfortable pace, staying in one place for a while, then magically moving forward as more learning takes place, you naturally come upon "it." "It" is total control in the water.

You become comfortable in water, shallow and deep, and begin to swim without effort. It's inevitable.

> *I can't imagine why this isn't the universal way swimming is taught.*
> — Margaret

Please let it happen. Tell yourself, "I don't have to push myself. Swimming will come to me naturally if I just take it easy and have fun." When something is uncomfortable, don't put up with it. Stop, and go back to what's comfortable. If it's uncomfortable, you must have skipped a step. Let yourself take your own comfortable path. It's your shortcut to success.

More fun learning

> ## STUDENTS' BILL OF RIGHTS
>
> In all classes, we hold these student rights to be inalienable:
>
> 1. The right to feel safe
> 2. The right to be comfortable
> 3. The right to ask all your questions
> 4. The right to receive correct answers
> 5. The right to learn at your own pace
> 6. The right to be taught by a qualified, knowledgeable instructor
> 7. The right to embody Step 1 before being presented with Step 2
> 8. The right to be supported
> 9. The right to share your experience with someone.

Step 17: Getting In

You've considered what you need to do in order to make your first (though it may not be your very first) foray into the pool. You've given yourself permission to stay true to yourself. You've gone to the pool of your choice. You're at the pool's shallow end.

Find a place to stop and take in the whole scene. What are your options for getting into the pool? Are there stairs? A ladder? Will you need to sit down and scoot off the edge?

Once you get in, you might just lean against the wall and watch what's happening. While you're there, notice your feelings and let them be there.

How is your heart rate? Normal? Elevated?

How is your breathing?

How is your "speed," that is, your internal vibration?

Do you feel tense inside or calm?

How is your balance? How is it when you're away from the wall?

All these measures in your body are signals. You wouldn't want to ignore them or override them. You'd want to be aware of them and let them be there. They are all okay. If something is uncomfortable, move to make yourself comfortable. Only then will you have attention to spare for learning.

Do this every time you get into the pool as a way to establish a safe and comfortable beginning, each day.

PRESSURE ON YOUR CHEST

Sometimes people feel pressure on their chests when they get into the water and submerge up to their shoulders. This is normal. If you don't feel it, that's fine. But if you do, it may feel as though your breathing is constricted. Stand up straighter or go to shallower water to relieve this feeling.

When you are in water, it exerts pressure on your body. You probably don't feel it anywhere except your chest. You feel it there because the air in your chest is less dense than water. You don't feel pressure on other parts of your body because the density of the rest of your body is closer to that of water.

Don't force yourself to be comfortable with this pressure on your chest. Proceed at your own pace. Stay happy and comfortable. If it sounds like fun, drop down so that your chest is under water again, and come back up before it gets uncomfortable. In other words, just feel it, and then come up. Rest. Do it again, if you're willing. Do it as long as you enjoy it. If this is what you learn today in the pool, it's enough.

STEP 18: LETTER TO THE WATER

Here's a rich exercise. To some people, the benefits of writing a letter to the water are obvious. Others think I'm nuts. Or they hope no one finds out what they're doing. I ask you to surrender and just do it. It'll help you. It's just for you.

Use a following page to write to the water as though it were a person. Write your feelings. Write your thoughts, positive, or negative, about shallow water, deep water, the drain, whatever. Write until you can write no more. Dump all your feelings out on the page. Use more paper if necessary (which is likely). You're walking around in the world with a lot of feelings, many negative, about the water. You don't need to carry these around. To write them down helps you to heal. The more you write, the less you'll carry afterward. Write it all. Take your time.

One of my students, a self-proclaimed "macho" retired Oakland, California police officer, wrote ten pages for his conversation with the water. Today he is one of our instructors.

Here are two sample letters from past students.

Sample 1, from Deborah:

Hello, Water,
It's me. You know I'm scared. You have never been a friend to me. You have taken me to the depths of darkness. You at the same time have shown me some really beautiful things. I've enjoyed your warmth and at the same time I was scared that you'd take it away. You've made me feel conflicting feelings such as happiness and fear. I've missed so many opportunities and joys because I am afraid of you.

Today I am taking control of my life. I am still afraid, but I am going to take control.

> I will not let anyone push me anymore.
> I will not leave my body to your satisfaction.
> I will remain in control in the here and now.
> I will master my feelings.

My emotions come from the following experiences:

1. Kyra trying to teach me to swim in a public pool. I felt uncomfortable because I didn't look good in my swimsuit, because too many people were in the pool, because the pool had urine in it, because people would laugh when they realized I couldn't swim. Because I stepped on glass and cut my foot. I was more afraid when I left the pool than before I got in.

2. Pepperdine University: Peter pushes me in the pool's deep end. I stay under until Mark pulls me out. I was so grateful I married him.

3. Swimming lessons with my six-year-old son. He learns, I get a staff infection.

4. Rafting in Sacramento. I get knocked out of the raft by a stranger. My boyfriend fishes me out. You guessed it. I married him, too.

5. Rafting in Brazil. Rafting was great. Then the tour guide got this brilliant idea to have everyone get out of the rafts and slide down the natural waterfall and go through a few rapids. It took me 30 minutes to realize I lost one of my contacts under the water. Now that I understand "leaving my body" I can tell you that I left my body the minute my feet were knocked from under me. I lost control. I didn't enjoy any of these incidents with water. They all caused pain and fear just when I thought I'd have some fun.

6. My sixth experience was the TSI introductory class I took in Berkeley. I was so scared I was 20 minutes late. I just stood outside the class trying to get the nerve to knock on the door. Finally a kid came by and said, "Lady, they're in there. I'll knock for you." He began to kick the door. It was opened by a black man. I was shocked he was my new instructor. Being African American, [I am, too], he was the last person I expected to see.

7. This was the beginning of my journey of learning to conquer my fear of water. You see before I went near the water again, I needed to admit I was scared. I readily admitted this when I read the

course description for this class. It was exciting yet scary. I met a friend at the class, another African American woman whom I had worked with in the past. We bonded. We enjoyed the class. Our instructor understood we were afraid. He talked to us for hours. He addressed all our fears. We felt comfortable and most of all, capable. When he finished talking and asked us to get in the pool, we were all raring to go. This was my best experience ever in the water. Why? Because I was not pushed, cut, hurt, shoved, or sick. Because it was warm, I was safe, I was in control. At the end of class I begged to stay. I was having fun.

Hello, Deb,
It's me, Water. I am not the enemy. I am not scary. I am just like air: I exist. You need me to live. I am not the cause of your bad experiences; look at your notes. I only exist to keep you alive. If you open up you'll see that I am not scary, I am nourishing, cleansing, enjoyable and good. If you weren't afraid you'd see that I am fun. That you need and like me. That together we could do all kinds of things. That if you trust me you can not be hurt by me. That others caused your fear. I just am.

Sample 2, from Will:

Dear Water,
I have feared and hated you much of my life as if you were to blame. I was convinced that if I gave myself to you, you'd be intent on doing me harm. Perhaps in a past life I drowned, and have carried that memory locked deep inside me. So, I turned away from you, put you out of my mind, and concerned myself with other pursuits. Perhaps fearing, hating, and ignoring you all this time has served some purpose, but I am at a loss to define it. Now, in calm and perhaps with greater wisdom, I see that I've cut myself off from half of the world's mysteries and wonders to see. I've begun visiting wonderful and mystical areas on land, but what of all that you have to offer? It calls to me, but as yet, I lack the confidence to pursue it. I realize now that you offer neither fear nor love. You just are, and my perception of you is my own creation. I have the power to change that perception by understanding more of myself and how I am when we are together. Perhaps you're just so vast that you care not whether I fear or love you. That, perhaps, I am insignificant in your eyes. That you could cause me to not trust you, but once again that would be of my own creation.

Yesterday, I found out that you would hold me up, something I never expected. Were you being benevolent? It would be nice to think so, but I am beginning to realize that just as you're in me with no intention, so am I naturally in you. Whether I float or not, or how well, is simply what's true for me. How I choose to accept and use that truth is up to me. And there's more to learn. So, whether you care or not, I offer my apology to you for the way I felt. You did nothing, and my experience has always been just my feelings and understanding of me, and me alone when I am around you.

Dear Will,
Apology accepted. But you're wrong about me. You believe I don't care, but the truth is, I care much. I call to all with a simple message, "Come, enjoy all the wonders and mysteries I enfold." It's true that relative to your physical existence, I am vast. You perhaps, at one time, saw tremendous power for harm in that expanse. And sometimes, terrible things happen, although not of my own intention. As you're a slave to your own feelings and beliefs, I too am a slave to the rotation of the Earth and Moon, the winds and the role I must play. I have neither the power to deliberately harm nor to help, therefore, I must entrust you to yourselves and your own strengths and weaknesses. But that never, in any way, diminishes my wishes for you in feeling comfortable with me. I look forward to seeing you soon.

Now it's your turn. What would you say to the water?

My Letter to Water

Then, when you've said it all, ask the water if it has a reply. No kidding. What would the water say back to you? Give it a try. You might learn something. It's just for you.

_____

_____

_____

_____

_____

_____

_____

_____

_____

_____

_____

_____

_____

_____

_____

_____

_____

_____

_____

_____

_____

_____

_____

_____

STEP 19: MIAMI TO SEATTLE

If you wanted to walk from Miami to Seattle, you could do it. Sure, it would take a while. Sure, you would need support. But if you had enough time, food, rest, shelter, and warmth, and you wanted to do it, you could. The journey from where you are now with your swimming to where you want to be is similar to a walk from Miami to Seattle. It might seem just as far, but it won't be. Just as that walk can be made wonderful and thoroughly enjoyable, so can the path to your complete freedom and competence in water. If you take one step at a time and stay comfortable, it's inevitable that you'll get there.

If, on your walk from Miami to Seattle, you tried to leave Topeka to go to Denver before you had gone from Miami to Atlanta, it would not work. It simply cannot be done. In the same way, it's not possible to, say, learn to tread water comfortably in the deep before you learn to *be* comfortable in the deep. And you cannot expect to learn to swim before you're at ease in water in general.

To try to do either of these is to skip a boatload of steps. I have observed that:

THE ONLY CAUSE OF PROBLEMS IS SKIPPING STEPS

Please check the truth of that statement for yourself.

No wonder swimming lessons didn't meet your expectations. You were trying to leave Boise while you were still in Miami.

Body in Miami, attention in Boise

However, if you start at Step 1 (of anything) and master it before going to Step 2, and you master Step 2 before going to Step 3 and continue this way, you can't possibly fail to reach your goals. This is the way I hope you'll proceed. Furthermore, Step 1 and Step 2 are not physical skills. They are steps of understanding and presence.

STEP 20: CHECKING THINGS OFF THE LIST VS. LEARNING THEM

Which would you rather do? Learn and "own" the skill of floating, or float once, show an instructor, have her check you off a list as having floated, and try to learn the next more advanced skill?

> *Learning means gaining a permanent new understanding of, and ease with a skill or idea. We're not interested in temporary gains. Learning happens when you're present to a new skill and you let yourself embody it. The skill then becomes a part of you. If you do it enough, it will become part of you for life.*

If you passed a swimming test to graduate from high school or college by being checked off the list for performing a task once—gritting your teeth, hanging on by your fingernails, holding your breath to the bursting point, and living till the end of it—did you really "pass" the swimming test? Surely you asked yourself, "What good is this?"

Many steps were skipped between where you were when you began your swimming and where you were said to be when you "passed" the swimming test. More steps were skipped between your swimming test and receiving carte blanche to graduate as "safe in the water." Obviously you were not safe in the water.

Many schools have dropped the swimming requirement to graduate. I believe that the elimination of this requirement was due to the lack of a successful swimming program for afraid students. Passing a swimming test was a well-intentioned idea but to back up these good intentions, there had to be a good program in place for beginning students to succeed. Sadly, it usually wasn't, and students didn't receive the benefit of the requirement.

Jeannie

When you look at Jeannie, would you say that she's calm? Where is she? She's "home." This is a photo of her in an advanced class she took with us in the ocean. Jeannie wasn't always this way. In fact, she quit high school to dodge the swimming requirement for graduation! Now she's one of our instructors.

Countless students have told us how they fudged passing their swimming requirement to graduate. One man went to the back of the line of students being tested and kept going to the back of the line until class was over. His instructor forgot to test him in the next class. A book could be filled with stories like these.

I presume that you would rather have taken a class that taught you how to be in control in water. *Then* you would have liked to learn how to swim. As you experiment with this or that skill in the water, give yourself time to get to know them. Each is rich. Doing them will teach you more than just a new physical skill. It will teach you about water and yourself in it. There's so much to absorb that's new. What's more, you can't do the same things on land.

"I'M TOO ADVANCED FOR THIS"

Some will say, "Oh, I know how to do this. Show me the bigger stuff." Many will say, "I am fine in shallow water. I love the water. But it's the deep water that I need to learn about. That's what scares me. Show me what to do in the deep."

It so happens that if you really knew yourself in shallow water and you really knew how shallow water worked, you would be eager to try things in deep water. If you're not eager to get into deep water, you need to learn what you don't know about shallow water. That is, find out what you don't know yet about the water and your body in it and learn how to stay in your body. This will allow you to be in control in any situation in shallow water. When you become confident in shallow water, your learner's mind will impishly suggest that you try the same things in deep water. And if you have truly mastered yourself in shallow water, you'll have no problem doing these things in deep water.

If you have tried any of the following exercises before and they haven't "worked," I suggest that what was missing for you was your complete presence. The goal now is to do each of the steps provided in this book with your complete presence of mind. When you have done this, you'll be in control of your little toe, your breath, your nose and your balance, in any position in the shallow water. When you have done it enough, you won't wonder; you'll know.

As you read through the following exercises, take time to practice each one. If something seems too elementary for you, read the steps to make sure you haven't missed any information. When you're certain that you own a step on a certain front and there's no possible learning left for you in it, go on to the next one. Go slowly. If there truly is no more you can learn about it, you will probably come upon your next step naturally.

STEP 21: YOUR BELIEFS ABOUT WATER

Put a checkmark next to the beliefs you hold. Check your gut-level beliefs, not your intellectual beliefs: imagine that you're in the water as you consider each one.

_____ If I put my face in water, I'll get water in my nose or mouth.

_____ It's dangerous when I get water in my nose or mouth.

_____ If I get water in my nose or mouth, I'll struggle, sputter, cough, and possibly drown.

_____ If water gets into my mouth, I'll swallow it.

_____ If I relax in water, I'll drop straight to the bottom like a stone.

_____ Sometimes I can't keep my presence of mind in deep water.

_____ I am not a floater.

_____ I know I can float.

_____ I am not a swimmer yet.

_____ I was born a swimmer.

_____ It would be unwise of me to relax in water.

_____ I have to push myself in order to learn to swim.

_____ If I relax in water, I might lose control.

_____ I may not have adequate lung capacity to swim.

_____ Deep water works differently than shallow water.

_____ My mind works differently in deep water than it does in shallow water.

_____ It would be unwise of me to relax in deep water.

_____ If I relax in deep water, something dreadful will happen.

_____ Each breath I take must be maximal in case I don't get another one.

_____ I can't control my body well in shallow water.

_____ I can't control my body well in deep water.

_____ A skill that works in the shallow end won't necessarily work in the deep end.

_____ If I want to learn to swim, I have to follow the swimming instructor's directions, even if I don't want to.

_____ To float correctly, my body should be horizontal.

_____ Being able to float depends on where the bottom is.

_____ Being able to do other skills depends on where the bottom is.

_____ A person can't get air if s/he's in deep water because there's no bottom to stand on.

_____ When I'm in deep water, I must move vigorously to stay afloat.

_____ In deep water, I need skills that I don't need in shallow water.

_____ In order to rest, I need the bottom or the side.

_____ It's harder to breathe in deep water than in shallow water.

_____ Shallow water is as dangerous as deep water.

_____ Shallow water won't hold me up.

_____ Deep water won't hold me up.

_____ The water is more powerful than I am.

_____ I need to be more physically fit than I am to learn to swim.

_____ The method in this book may work for others but it may not work for me.

_____ I don't trust myself in deep water.

DO YOU HAVE OTHER BELIEFS ABOUT YOURSELF AND THE WATER?

List them here:

_____

_____

_____

Given that you have these beliefs, what would you expect your experience in the water to be like?

_____

_____

_____

Would you expect that you would feel free in deep water? Of course not. And if you keep these beliefs, do you think you'll learn to be confident and free in water? No.

> *Your beliefs and feelings are okay, no matter what they are. You have to start somewhere. If you try to start from where you wish you were, or where you think you should be, which is ahead of where you actually are, you'll skip steps. The way you're "supposed" to feel is the way you will feel once you allow yourself to feel the way you do feel.*

You've come to this book to learn how to have the beliefs you want to have. True? You want to believe that water holds you up, that you can be at ease without worry, that you can remain in control, that swimming is fun even in deep water. You want to feel that you can enjoy being in a pool, a lake, on a raft, in the ocean, or on (and off) a boat.

> Alice laughed. "There's no use trying," she said. One can't believe impossible things."
>
> "I dare say you haven't had much practice," said the Queen. "When I was your age I always did it for half an hour a day. Why, sometimes, I've believed as many as six impossible things before breakfast."
> —*Through the Looking Glass*
> Lewis Carroll

In order to *have* the experiences you want to have, you need to be able to *do* things differently. In order to be able to *do* those things differently (for example, the way you lie on the water, or put your face in, or move through the water) you need to *believe* differently. You therefore want to change your beliefs. Do you agree? You want to change the way you're *being* about the water or deep water.

STEP 22: BEING/DOING/HAVING

At the core of you is you, a spirit. This is pure goodness, light, peacefulness, wisdom and knowledge. This is my belief. Is it yours? It helps explain my entire thesis, all of my work. It is demonstrated by 100% of my students.

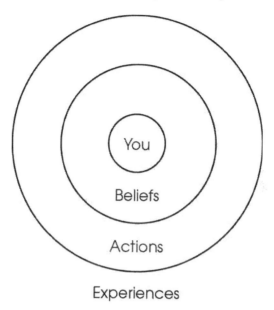

Experiences

Just outside the core of you, are your beliefs. It's your beliefs that determine how you will "be" in the world. Your beliefs come from what you're taught by others, or from your interpretation of your experiences. Your beliefs about your safety cause you to be either at ease in the water or tense in the water.

If your beliefs about being in deep water are scary, you'll be scared in the water. When you believe that water holds you up, or that you can remain in control in deep water, you'll no longer be afraid.

Just beyond your beliefs are the things you *do*. These things you *do*, you *do* because of the beliefs you have. Your actions come from your beliefs. You *do* as you believe.

For example, if you believe that water does not hold you up, then you'll struggle to stay up to prevent yourself from sinking. Or, to try to prove to yourself that water does hold you up, you may struggle to keep your feet off the bottom. Both of these involve struggle.

If you believe that water does hold you up, you'll let your (hands and) feet go where they naturally go when gravity and buoyancy have their say.

From the things you *believe* come the things you *do*. From the things you *do* come the results you *have*. Therefore, what you *have* comes from what you *believe*. Your experiences come from your beliefs.

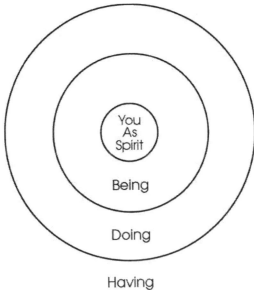

If you want to *have* the *experience* of freedom in water, your beliefs need to support your being free. This next exercise puts in motion the process to change your beliefs.

Go through this list again. After each belief, re-write it, stating clearly what you *want* to believe.

If I put my face in water, I'll get water in my nose or mouth.

_____

It's dangerous when I get water in my nose or mouth.

_____

If I get water in my nose or mouth, I'll struggle, sputter, cough, and possibly drown.

_____

If water gets into my mouth, I'll swallow it.

_____

If I relax in water, I'll drop straight to the bottom like a stone.

_____

Sometimes I can't keep my presence of mind in deep water.

_____

I am not a floater.

_____

I know I can float.

_____

I am not a swimmer yet.

_____

I was born a swimmer.

It would be unwise of me to relax in water.

I have to push myself in order to learn to swim.

If I relax in water, I might lose control.

I may not have adequate lung capacity to swim.

Deep water works differently than shallow water.

My mind works differently in deep water than it does in shallow water.

It would be unwise of me to relax in deep water.

If I relax in deep water, something dreadful will happen.

Each breath I take must be maximal in case I don't get another one.

I can't control my body well in deep water.

If a skill works in the shallow end, it won't necessarily work in the deep end.

_____

If I want to learn to swim, I have to follow the swimming instructor's directions, even if I don't want to.

_____

To float correctly, my body should be horizontal.

_____

Being able to float depends on where the bottom is.

_____

Being able to do other skills depends on where the bottom is.

_____

A person can't get air if s/he's in deep water because there's no bottom to stand on.

_____

When I'm in deep water, I must move vigorously to stay afloat.

_____

In deep water, I need skills that I don't need in shallow water.

_____

In order to rest, I need the bottom or the side.

_____

It's harder to breathe in deep water than in shallow water.

_____

Melon Dash

Shallow water is as dangerous as deep water.

Shallow water won't hold me up.

Deep water won't hold me up.

The water is more powerful than I am.

I need to be more physically fit than I am to learn to swim.

This book may work for others but it may not work for me.

I don't trust myself in deep water.

Other beliefs you want to have:

By becoming aware of these beliefs—both the ones you have and the ones you want to have—a slight shift takes place. Can you feel it? It's a physical shift. Even though your body may not have "moved," something inside you moved the tiniest bit.

74

Step 23: Your Face

> *"Last night I put my face in the shower for the first time in my life!"*
> -- Annabella, age 56

Q: What do you do if you drop the soap in the shower?
A: Kick it to the other end of the tub and get it.

How do you feel at the thought of putting your face in the water? Feel your body's reaction. If you tense up, feel where the tension is. Feel it for a few minutes. Then rest. Just do what's fun.

Think again about putting your face in, and let the tension be there. When you let it be there, what happens? Let it be there until it lessens and then disappears. Go slowly and be gentle. Don't push yourself.

Without getting into the water, you can practice putting your face in, by repeatedly thinking about it and feeling your reaction. Repeat this until you can think about it and remain comfortable.

What are your concerns, if any, about having your face in water? Here are some common ones:

- Water in the nose
- Water in the eyes
- Water in the mouth
- Water in the ears
- Inhaling water
- Running out of air
- Losing balance
- Losing control/panicking
- Not being able to come up in time for air
- Feeling claustrophobic

Let's take care of every single one of these so you can trust putting your face in water.

WE DON'T CARE IF YOU ACTUALLY PUT YOUR FACE IN

When I say we, I mean you and me. What we care about is that you feel completely in control. Do you agree?

MAKING IT SAFE TO PUT YOUR FACE IN

Look at a second hand on a watch or clock. If you can hold your breath for five seconds, you can imagine feeling safe putting your face in the water for one second. True? Take a breath and time how long you can hold it.

This gives you an idea of how long you can comfortably have your face in the water. For almost all of the skills you learn in this book in which your face is in the water, you'll be holding your breath. This is the best way for you to come to know your lung capacity and the amount of time you can "play" on that much air. Later in the book we'll introduce breathing but for now, just become very familiar with holding your breath. Always keep it comfortable. Don't push yourself at all. In fact, I'm counting on you *not to.*

Please don't expect to remember all the steps below when you go to the pool. I wouldn't ask you to. Get the idea of what is meant as you read, and then do what your body tells you when you're at the pool. In case you get stuck, you may want to take the book along. You can also practice some of these skills in a tub that's not too hot. Ninety-five degrees Fahrenheit (35° C) is okay. One hundred and two degrees (hot tub) is rather hot for your face (39°C).

Do all of the following, which will help you to feel 100% safe putting your face in the water. Doing fewer of the following is not more advanced than doing all of them. The most advanced result is feeling 100% in control: no discomfort.

- Hold onto the wall or gutter with one hand

- Hold your nose

- Take a breath

- Close your mouth

- Close your eyes

- Slowly lower yourself down toward the water. There's no need to put your ears under water but if you want to, it's okay.

- As you approach the water's surface, ask yourself if putting your face in is what you really want to do (sounds like fun). If some part of you is saying, "No," then come back up. Take a break. When you feel rested, start again. Repeat this cycle as many times as necessary until you reach the point where you *want* to put your face in. *We don't care if you put your face in.* We only care that you're practicing staying in control. The more you practice control, the better you'll be at remaining in control. After a while, you become expert at remaining in control. And after that, you'll feel free and safe to put your face in.

- If you want to put your face in, then hold your breath and slowly lower your face into the water, keeping your hand on your nose and your eyes and mouth closed. Spend a moment there, while it's comfortable.

- Come up whenever you want to. Don't push yourself to stay down. You may be there for one second. If this feels like enough for you, it is enough.

- Practice this many, many times, or as many as you can enjoy.

By the Way: Holding Air in Your Cheeks

Often, as someone prepares to go under water, he holds air in his cheeks.

Cheeks full of air (with a bubble sneaking out).

Getting ready to submerge, he's sure he wants air, but the air he needs isn't in his cheeks.

The air in your cheeks isn't available for your body to use. It just puffs up your cheeks. The air you live on is in your lungs. So, when you take a breath and hold it, feel it in your lungs. Your face doesn't have to work.

Claustrophobia in the Water

Some students feel closed-in under water. The claustrophobic students have all overcome their fear of putting their faces in water. You may not believe me now, and that's fine.

It's true that you can't breathe in with your face in the water. You can breathe out if you wish (but it's not necessary now). Your lungs can hold so much air that there's plenty to live on for every exercise we will do. Later you'll learn that it's hard to get rid of all your air even if you want to.

I won't try to talk you out of claustrophobia. I just ask you to listen to your feelings and experiment with the steps provided, at your own pace. And stay true to yourself.

Your lungs can hold enough air for you to go into the water and come back up and still have loads of air left. Are you willing to test this?

You can heal the sensation of claustrophobia in the water. Follow your instinct. If it says, "Don't go in," don't go in. Just go as far as you feel completely comfortable going. Make sure you hold onto the wall. Make sure you hold your nose. Allow yourself to do only what you can do while staying in your body. Give yourself many days to learn to put your face in. Let go of a timetable. If you stay in your body and let go of a timetable, you'll learn.

STEP 24: THE NECESSITY OF BEING IN CONTROL

WHY IT'S MORE IMPORTANT TO BE IN CONTROL THAN TO DO A SKILL

People have asked, "Are you sure you don't want me to force my face in, just to get it done?" Yes, I'm sure.

Why put your face in if you don't want to? You don't have to do things you don't like to do in order to learn to swim. If you did, why would you *want* to learn to swim? You'd be practicing the third circle, which is not a skill or a behavior you want to learn.

You're already experienced enough at pushing and losing control. Our goal is to experience control and comfort. You're reading this book because you want to know how to be in control all the time in the water, shallow and deep, in the middle or at the side, at the surface or the bottom of the pool, and perhaps in the lake or ocean. You want to be in control whether someone splashes you or not, jumps in right next to you, bumps into you, or whether you walk off a drop-off or fall from a dock or boat. True?

You may have thought that you would get control by learning swim skills. The truth is, you'll get control by practicing control. You'll build confidence in your ability to stay in control by starting with little successes and building on them. You'll swim when you feel so in-control that you then have attention to spare for what to do with your arms, legs and breath.

Practice putting your face in the water 50 to 100 times, as described several pages back. Give yourself all the time in the world. You aren't in a hurry, are you? If so, you're at least in the second circle. This won't work in the long run. Stop and come back home to your body.

> ## 2+2=4
> TO LEARN, YOU MUST BE ABLE TO DO STEP 1 AND REMAIN IN THE FIRST CIRCLE EVERY TIME, BEFORE YOU CAN ADD STEP 2.

WHAT IS YOUR FACE DOING?

Once you've had your face in water for a while, notice your expression under water. What are the sensations in your face? Your forehead? Eyes? Cheeks? Mouth? Jaw?

Tension is okay: find it, feel it, and *let it be there*. Catch yourself if you're thinking, "I should relax." Having tension in your face uses energy and attention, even if you don't notice it. If some of your attention and energy are in your face, then *all of you* can't be learning the next step. Let all your attention be in your face while your face requires it. It's okay: go with it.

If you ever feel stuck during this learning process, check back to see if you're in the first circle. If there's tension, meaning you're in the second or third circle, you won't be able to advance in that skill. Go back and find where any tension is, and *let it be there*. Don't expect progress unless and until you've allowed it fully, which gives it it's first chance to disappear.

ARE YOU SWALLOWING WHILE YOU'RE UNDER WATER?

Sometimes, people find themselves swallowing when they put their faces in the water. This is okay. They're not swallowing water…they're simply swallowing. If you find yourself swallowing, let it happen. There's no harm in it. By allowing it, you'll eventually see what you're doing to cause it. Then you'll get control over it. Later, when you have even more control, it will stop by itself.

This is "honest learning" as I call it, an organic change that happens naturally and without force.

While we're on the topic of swallowing, let's establish this: if you do find yourself swallowing water, it's not dangerous. It goes into your stomach, as it would if you were drinking from a glass. You can swallow a lot of water, even many gulps in a row if things are not going as planned, and not be in danger from the water intake. If you're swallowing water because you're out of control, it's being out of control that could lead to danger, not the water intake. Once again, being in control is the key skill to learn.

If, however, you're in water that's not clean, you wouldn't want to swallow it. You shouldn't even get into it. If you have a sense that the water at the pool isn't clean or if you're not sure, don't get in. It's okay to ask, though you could get an odd look.

If you're in the ocean, swallowing a lot of salt water can be distressing and may make you nauseous after a while. Remember that this happens when you aren't in control. This is why it is so important to master remaining in control. When you learn to be in your body, it's unlikely that swallowing water will happen anymore.

STEP 25: PUTTING YOUR EARS IN

It's safe to get water in your ears. For all intents and purposes, your ears are like side pockets in your head. Water won't go into your brain, nose or throat. If you're not comfortable putting your ears in water, follow this recipe:

- Hold onto the wall with one or both hands.

- Tip your head sideways, parallel to the surface.

- Lower your head.

- As you approach the surface with one ear, ask yourself whether you want to put your ear in the water or not. Is there any tension in your body telling you, "No"? If so, come up and take a break.

- If not, anticipate the feeling of putting your ear in: your hearing will change (sounds will be muffled in that ear). Your ear will fill up with water, which may tickle a bit.

- You can just touch your earlobe to the water and see how that feels. If you don't like the idea of submersing your ear, come back up and take a break.

- Once you're willing to put your ear in, see how it feels. See how *your body* feels with your ear in. Come up whenever you want to.

> WE DON'T CARE IF YOU PUT YOUR EAR IN THE WATER. WE ONLY CARE THAT YOU HAVE FUN AND REMAIN IN CONTROL.

When you get into the water to actually try this, I hope you won't say to yourself, "Oh, I can skip that step. She doesn't really mean that." I am giving you the tried and true, the guaranteed-to-be-successful steps. If you want to give yourself the best possible chance for success, follow the steps. If you *know* that you don't need a step though, trust yourself. You're right.

Once you've become comfortable with submersing one ear, follow the same steps with your other ear. Take your time. Don't push yourself. Remain in the first circle.

How to get water out of your ears

- Sometimes, water doesn't all drain out of your ears when you come to the surface. Shaking your head usually gets rid of it. If a gentle shake doesn't do it, then:

- move your head quickly in one direction and then stop it. The water will keep going.

- If that doesn't clear your ears, go back under water and fill your ears again. Come back up and try the same thing.

- If that doesn't clear them, put a drop of mineral oil in your ear. Use only mineral oil. Lie on your side with your head on a pillow (or not) and wait 5 minutes. It should clear.

Taking Care of Your Ears

After swimming, allow your ears to dry. If you have long hair, put it behind your ears until they air-dry. You would not want to place your head down on a pillow and go to sleep when your ear is still wet. You could wake up with Swimmers' Ear, a fungal infection. If you need to dry your ears quickly, remember the saying: "Never put anything smaller than your elbow in your ear." Hold a hair dryer at arm's length from your ear and direct the air toward it.

When you feel okay about putting each of your ears in, hold the wall and ask yourself if you're ready to try putting your head under water far enough that both ears go in. If that doesn't sound like fun, feel where the tension is in your body when you just imagine it. Let yourself feel that tension. Don't try to make it disappear: it has a message of protection for you. When you've let it be there, the tension will start to melt away. This is simply the way it works. If you're in a hurry, you'll delay your learning. If it's not time to put your ears in, that's fine.

$2+2=4$
WHEN YOU ALLOW TENSION TO BE THERE,
IT HAS ITS FIRST OPPORTUNITY TO DISAPPEAR—AND IT WILL

We don't know if it will leave right now or not, but at least you're giving it a chance. You aren't in control of *when* it disappears. You just have to allow it. Then it will go. This is an "energy law:" one of the laws that governs the way energy works. This is why it's important *not* to be in a hurry when you learn. You, as a spirit are energy.

TENSION IS A COMMUNICATION

When your body is tense, you're receiving a message from your beliefs that you may not be safe. It would be crazy to proceed if you actually are not safe. The part of you that believes you're not safe is the part of you that is learning and overcoming fear. To overcome fear, you must pay attention to the beliefs and the tension. When your body believes that you're safe because you're listening to it and letting tension be there, tension disappears. Your belief starts to change. You grow. Listen to your body. It's the communication channel between your wisdom and you.

Have you ever been told by swimming teachers and family members to relax in the water?

Being told to relax is practically a joke for afraid students.

If you try to make tension disappear ("RELAX!"), it usually persists. *What you resist persists.*

We don't want you to be tense, since tension means you're not having fun and you're in the second circle or beyond. At the same time, we don't want you to tell yourself to relax because sometimes that helps you relax and sometimes it makes you tense up. We need a system that gives you the best chance of regaining control every single time.

The system to learn is this: let yourself be the way you are. By letting yourself be tense, your resistance to tension goes away. Then, your tension can also go away. This is a most effective solution. It heals.

If at some time in the future you find yourself in a frightening situation and you *cannot* make yourself relax, you will still be able to pull through because you will have developed a far more dependable habit: letting yourself be the way you are. Practice this.

You'll automatically begin to relax once you allow what's already happening to happen. Tension is okay. Your trusting it will heal it. Don't be in a hurry to change. The change happens by itself when you're in your body. Change doesn't happen if you're next to your body, pushing. *I know I've said this many times.* Hopefully you're learning it. If I've said it too much, please pardon me.

STEP 26: COMPARING YOURSELF TO OTHERS

To compare yourself to others, or to compare yourself to your vision of where you "should be," is to be outside of yourself, looking back at yourself. Being outside of your body, you're in no position to learn. You may even be in an attack position: ready to judge yourself if you don't measure up to someone else. Is this going to help you learn?

If you're comparing yourself, bring yourself back into your body, and feel your feelings. Impatience? Sadness? Tension? Hurry? Just be still and feel them. They have a place in your learning and healing. Just feel as much as you feel safe to feel. Let that energy/emotion be there and let it move. This is the definition of healing!

When you recover from comparing yourself, consider walking across the pool. You might imagine yourself holding onto the wall, or doing whatever makes you feel safe. When you're ready to try it, go slowly, the safest way. Feel. Feel what it's like to be in the exact same place that your body is, to fill your body with your presence from head to toe and fingertip to fingertip. If you do this, you're likely to feel things you haven't felt before in water. You may feel your buoyancy. Sometimes people feel the resistance of the water, which is so much greater than that of air. Sometimes people feel how their balance is different than in air. All these are factors to learn about.

Control is all that matters. (Fun matters too, but you have to be in control in water to have fun.)

STEP 27: OPENING YOUR EYES UNDER WATER

We don't care if you open your eyes or not. What we care about is that you feel comfortable and in control. Most people want to be able to see in the water. Many have never opened their eyes below the surface. If you wear goggles or a mask (to be described in a moment), opening your eyes under water is easy.

Many people want to know what it's like to open their eyes without goggles or a mask, so they'll be familiar with this feeling. They want to know that if they ever fall into the water without goggles, they won't "lose it." Good idea. If putting your eyes into the water and opening them sounds like no fun at all, skip this part for now. Keep them closed or wear goggles. Please do not pry your eyes open or force them. Simply let them open when they are ready.

When you put your face into water, notice whether there's tension in your eyes. Go ahead and see. If you find tension in your eyes, practice what you're learning: let it be there. Just feel the tension. Don't tell yourself to relax. Don't force your eyes open. When you have allowed tension to be there, what do you think will happen? Write it here: _____

The tension in your eyes starts to disappear, or your eyes open. If not, feel and allow the tension again. You'll notice that it requires just the slightest bit of tension to keep your eyes closed. If you allow *that* tension, what happens? Your eyes open *on their own*. You can see. It will be blurry, but you can see.

How does it feel on your eyeballs to open your eyes? Only open them as much as you want to. It's just for fun. It won't hurt you. The view is blurry because there's no air space in front of your eyes. If you were to wear goggles, your vision would be as clear as it is in the air. Look around under water. Can you see other people's legs? The colors of their suits? The number of fingers I'm holding up? Just kidding.

If you were to leave your eyes open for 5-10 minutes in most chlorinated pools, they might burn a little bit from the chemical balance. This doesn't cause damage, but it can be uncomfortable. This is the reason so many people use goggles. They provide good vision and comfort for your eyes. Pools that have ozonated water (and therefore less chlorine) don't sting your eyes.

It's good to spend some time in the pool with your face in the water and your eyes open every day so it becomes natural and comfortable. After it becomes second nature to you to open your eyes under water, you may wish to get a pair of goggles (see below). It's fine to spend all your time in the water without goggles, but they make it possible to see much better. Seeing clearly gives more control.

GLASSES

If you can't see well without your glasses, and taking them off makes you uncomfortable in the water, there are several things you can do.

- Wear them in the pool. This only works while you're above the surface.

- Wear contacts under goggles.

- Purchase goggles that have your prescription ground into the lenses.

STEP 28: MAKE IT SIMPLE FOR YOURSELF

It won't hurt you to make things simple. This will assist you in being in your body, which is the whole point. Make *everything* simple. There is no such thing as "cheating" as you learn to swim. Get the basic concerns out of the way (fear, cold, water in your nose…). When you don't have to worry about these things, you can learn what you want to know. Learn how to be comfortable first.

CHOOSING AND USING A NOSE CLIP

A nose clip is a small device that keeps water out of your nose, frees your hands, and therefore gives you more control. Many people think of it as a crutch. Others consider it "cheating." In truth, it's neither a crutch nor cheating: it helps you to be in your body. Why not make it easy for yourself? A nose clip is a steppingstone. You'll stop using it when the time is right, when you don't need it anymore.

A nose clip can be anything from a clothespin to an $8 colored designer item. Nose clips usually cost $3-$5. Different brands have different shapes, and one will fit your nose better than others. Nose clips will fall off if you have sun block on your nose. You may have to invest a few dollars and use trial and error to find the best one.

Once you have a nose clip, test it to make sure it stays on your face and no water enters your nose. Found a good one? Buy two. Please give yourself permission to use a nose clip if it will help you stay in your body. It's more important to stay in control than to be nose-clip-free.

CHOOSING GOGGLES

Goggles are small, enclosed glasses that provide air space in front of your eyes so you can see clearly under water. There are hundreds of models of goggles on the market. They fit all kinds of faces. A great pair for me could be a pair that doesn't work at all for you. Find a pair that fits your face comfortably and doesn't leak.

To find a pair of goggles, go to a swimming-supply or sporting goods store and ask if they have unpackaged goggles you can try on. If not, they may let you open packages.

Placing the goggles against your face without the strap around your head, press them into your eye sockets and see if they create suction. If they do, they are likely to fit you. If they are the type that doesn't rely on suction, it will say so on the package; follow the instructions for fitting. Most goggles are the suction type.

If you want vision correction in your goggles, there are models that are ground to a certain diopter. You can buy them over the counter at many swimming gear and sporting goods stores. Some optometrists grind goggles to match your exact prescription. Check to see which models can be ground, then choose one that fits your face.

There are also several types of masks, larger and for some people more comfortable than goggles, that don't cover the nose. Ask to try on a swimmer's mask. You can't be sure until you get into the pool whether or not a pair will be leak-proof. Ask at the store about their return policy.

Once you begin to wear goggles, review from time to time opening your eyes under water without them. This helps you to practice control without goggles. If you were ever to find yourself in the water without goggles, you'd want to know that you wouldn't lose control just because you didn't have them.

"Using goggles and a nose clip really made a difference for me and made me feel very comfortable."
—Joseph

STEP 29: THE SPIRITUAL SIDE OF LEARNING

THERE'S NO SUCH THING AS "STUCK"

All things in the universe are composed of energy in one form or another. Your body is energy, your thoughts are energy, sound and light are energy, information is energy, emotion is energy. Your chair is energy.

Energy does only two things: it expands and contracts Everything in the universe expands and contracts. Though you may not be able to detect it, your chair expands and contracts in a rhythm of its own. Your heart expands and contracts in a rhythm of its own. So do the molecules of this page. And though we don't yet have instruments sophisticated enough to measure them, your moods and learning expand and contract in their own rhythm.

You may say, "I've experienced my energy expanding when I feel good. I feel myself contracting when I feel bad. But I have also felt stuck. Isn't that a third thing that energy does?" No. "Stuck" can only happen if there's contraction. Energy keeps expanding unless there's contraction.

Contraction is part of the cycle of learning. It's not bad or good: it just is. We contract when it's necessary to "keep ourselves safe" according to our beliefs.

How does this relate to your swimming? When you're in the water and you're worried, how does your body feel? What does it do? It contracts—gets tense. Your chin may come down, your shoulders may hunch up, and your chest, throat, arms, legs, and jaw may tighten.

On the other hand, when you're in water and you feel safe, how does your body feel? You're relaxed, expanded. You feel looser, more at ease. You expand your body by thinking calming, soothing thoughts. You contract by thinking scary, threatening thoughts.

You may have never thought of having control over which thoughts you had in the water. And you may not have had any. But today, please open to this possibility: when you're on land and you notice yourself having scary thoughts and tensing up, check your thoughts. Are those the thoughts you want to have? If yes, fine. If no, fine. Are they based in truth? If yes, fine. If no, fine. Be aware that you have a choice about what you want to think next.

When you're *in the water* and you find yourself becoming tense, check your thoughts. Are those the thoughts you want to have? If yes, fine. If no, fine. Are they based in truth? If yes, fine. If no, fine. Just be aware that you have a choice.

I'm not asking you to talk yourself out of being tense. I am asking you to choose. You can steer your thoughts out of the encroaching grip of panic if you don't like them. To steer your thoughts is to change your "location." It's simply another tool in your toolbox to bring you closer to the truth about yourself in the water. You are energy. Your thoughts determine whether you expand or contract. Your body and your thoughts together give you fabulous clay with which to mold the swimmer you were born to be. This molding can happen with fun and very little effort.

> ## GO SLOWLY ENOUGH THAT YOU CAN BE CONSCIOUS OF YOUR CHOICES

EXERCISE: PRESENCE

Where you are now? Are you in your body? Are you partly in your body and partly somewhere else? Are you totally "gone?" No. You'd have to reread the paragraph if you were gone.

Here is an exercise that you can do with someone else. Ask him to read it to you:

- Bring your focus into your body fully. Feel what it's like to be totally "home." Is this where you spend most of your day? Part of your day? Any of your day? (Just kidding.)

- Now close your eyes and feel yourself sitting in your seat. Come home. Be aware of your sitting position, the clothes you're wearing, the way they feel on your body, and your sensations.

- Now pretend that you're across the room looking back at your body. It's sitting in the chair. See the position it's in and what it's wearing.

- Then, bring yourself back into your body again. You're home again. How does it feel?

- Now imagine yourself again across the room, looking back at your body sitting in the chair. Look at it from across the room.

- Now return to your body again and feel what it's like to be in it.

It feels different to be in your body than to be across the room. Did you feel it? This is a good exercise to teach you the different feelings between being in your body and being out. Don't worry if you were not able to do it. Not everyone can.

When you're in the water, you can keep your energy in your body by *feeling*. Feel how the water embraces every inch of your body. Feel how it buffets you ever so slightly back and forth or holds you as you simply stay still. Feel your arms' lightness in the water. Feel how much air you have. By keeping your attention (your focus, yourself) in your body, you remain in the present, in control. It's simple. It works.

There is more to the spiritual side of learning. We have touched on some of it already. The physical side includes your body, gravity, buoyancy, the amount of air you hold. The spiritual side includes how energy works, your beliefs, thoughts, and feelings. It includes your compassion toward yourself and your permission to go slowly. More on these later.

For those who are challenged by this message, here is one student's comment:

> *It sounds like b--------, but it works.*
>
> —Tim

STEP 30: PUTTING YOUR FACE IN WITHOUT HOLDING YOUR NOSE

When you put your head in the water earlier (face and ears), you either held your nose or you didn't. If you did, and you'd like to keep your nose sealed off, you can either hold it or use a nose clip. If you use your hand, your nose will obviously be safe. However, using your hand occupies that hand.

If you prefer not to use a nose clip, you can learn to keep water out of your nose in front float positions. Holding your nose, put your face in the water as you have been doing it. Once there, while you're feeling completely in control—and if it sounds like fun—add one new thing: release your grip on your nose, keeping your hand right in the same spot. Don't change anything but that one small thing: letting go of your nose. You won't get water in your nose. You won't inhale, because you're present and you're only doing one thing. You'll find that it's safe to have your nose unplugged in the water.

Note: if you're thinking you don't want to use a nose clip because in the long run you don't want to wear one, please reconsider. Today is not the long run. Today is "comfort priority day." Do what will make you most comfortable today. What you want for the long run will take care of itself.

When you take your hand off your nose under water, the pressure of your fingers on your nose goes away (I don't mean to be too elementary here). Your nostrils fill with water. This is not the same as "getting water up your nose." Having your nostrils fill with water is possibly a new sensation and for some people it takes a few minutes of practice for several days to get used to it. When water takes up the space in your nostrils, it fills your nostrils, just as it would fill an empty glass if you placed it in the water. See if the sensation is okay with you. Get accustomed to this new feeling.

Please be kind to yourself. There's no hurry. Practice having your face under water with your hand an inch from your nose. If you feel comfortable with that, and you know that you won't inhale because you're in control, feel what it's like to have your face in water, nose open. Practice this thirty times. One hundred times. No hurry.

When you become comfortable having your nose free, you'll be able to move your hand away from your face and know that your nose is safe. Your nose is safe because you know what you're doing: you're *there*.

The sensation of "getting water up your nose" is actually getting water in your sinuses. The bones around your nose form a circle at the top of your nose, beyond which your sinuses lie. If water goes beyond this circle, it enters your sinuses. We want to avoid this whenever possible because it's quite uncomfortable. You would not want to become accustomed to the discomfort of getting water in your sinuses because:

1) if you are uncomfortable, you're a step closer to the fifth circle

2) too much water in the nose (sinuses) can cause a sinus infection

Smile: you can prevent water from going beyond the circle at the back of your nose and into your sinuses.

94

STEP 31: HOW TO KEEP WATER OUT OF YOUR NOSE

As long as your head doesn't tip backward or upside down, and if you don't inhale through your nose when it's under water, the water in your nostrils will not get into your sinuses. If your face is tilted straight down or straight ahead in the water, all the water in your nostrils will stay in your nostrils and cause no discomfort. If your head is in one of the following positions, you will not get water into your sinuses (your "nose") unless, of course, you inhale—in other words, if you're not home. Safe positions for your nose:

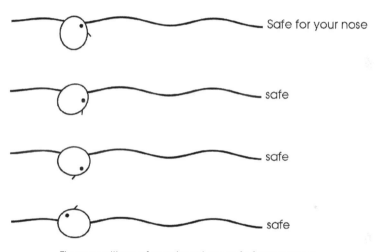

These positions of your head are safe for your nose

However, if you...

1. turn upside down,

2. do a somersault,

3. look upward while under water, or

4. put your head backward too far while you're in a back float, the water sitting in your nostrils will go into your sinuses unless you know how to prevent it. You'll probably come up and sneeze.

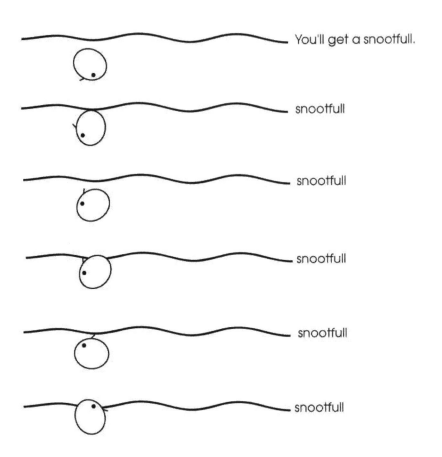

You'll get a snootfull.

snootfull

snootfull

snootfull

snootfull

snootfull

Uncomfortable positions for your nose:
If your head is in any of these positions, you will get a snootfull.

You can prevent getting water in your nose by:

- Not tipping your head backward or putting it upside down

- Not inhaling when you're under water (this means you must "be there")

- Not moving your nose through the water like a scoop

- Using a nose clip

- Holding your nose

- Exhaling through your nose anytime your head is tipping backward or going upside down. It's completely safe and comfortable to be upside down or turning somersaults in the water. You won't get water in your nose *if,* as you turn, you exhale through your nose. The air coming out of your nose will prevent water from coming in. Exhaling through your mouth will not keep water out of your nose.

BLIPPING

Here is another way to keep water out of your nose. Inhale through your mouth above the surface, then exhale a little bit of air through your nose as you put your face in. Stop exhaling after your nose is below the surface. I call this sending out a "blip" of air. Just a few bubbles outward prevent you from getting water inward. If you "blip" each time you put your face in and take your face out, you'll prevent water from coming into your nose. If you don't blip, you may not get water into your nose, either…but if you want to ensure no water, blip.

Blipping: just exhale a couple of bubbles, then stop.

Give yourself lots of time to become comfortable with blipping: days.

This habit of blipping to keep water out of your nose is worth every minute you put into it. I urge you to give yourself enough time to practice and embody it, or, give yourself permission to use a nose clip (unless water isn't entering your sinuses). Avoid discomfort.

Once you can have your hands free of your nose and you're at ease with your face in the water, you'll be ready for another step. But don't try to move on until you're happy having your face and ears in the water.

KEEP YOUR NOSE HAPPY AT ALL TIMES

STEP 32: REVIEW

Every time you get into the water, review the basics you have already covered. Remove expectations that you'll surpass the point you reached last time so there will be no pressure. Then practice:

1. noticing how you feel

2. allowing yourself to be "where you are" today with no expectations of repeating what you did yesterday

3. letting yourself be yourself

4. putting your face in

5. putting your ears in

6. asking yourself if this is enough for today

7. doing whatever would be fun

8. if you're in the mood to continue practicing, then practice...

9. taking your hand off your nose

10. opening your eyes under water

STEP 33: FEELING THE WATER HOLDING YOU UP ON YOUR FRONT: THE FRONT FLOAT

Once you're comfortable (in the first circle) putting your face and ears in the water, you may wish to learn how to float. The first step of floating is feeling that the water holds you up. To assure yourself that you're safe, hold onto the wall and *don't let go*...unless, of course, you're already comfortable without the wall.

> **DON'T EVEN THINK ABOUT LETTING GO OF THE WALL**

> *"This is one swimming class where they encourage you not to let go of the wall."*
>
> -- KTVU News, Oakland, CA, 1995

Face the wall and hold onto it with both hands. Promise yourself you won't let go.

Take a comfortable breath. When you're ready, put your face in the water and let your body just dangle in the water as you hold onto the wall. Let your feet be where they are on the floor of the pool. Don't try to make your body become horizontal, or raise your feet off the floor. If they float up by themselves, that's fine. If not, fine. Do you believe me? You don't have to push yourself into a horizontal position. You don't have to push yourself below the surface, either. Just lie there limply, letting your body dangle while holding onto the wall. The more air you have the higher you'll float. If you can leave your feet on the floor, do so.

Here is a stick drawing of a good front float by someone who is allowing the water to do all the work.

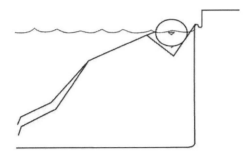

A good front float at the wall

A FLOAT DOES <u>NOT</u> HAVE TO BE HORIZONTAL

Contrary to popular belief, a good float is not *supposed* to be horizontal, whether it's a front float or a back float. A good float is one in which your body does no work, and the water does it all. All you do is hold your breath. For some people (some bodies), the float will be horizontal.

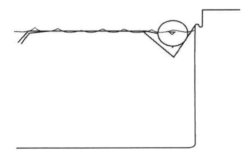

Another good front float at the wall

Some people float vertically:

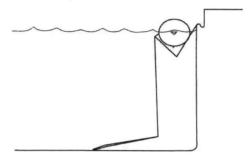

Some people may not float:

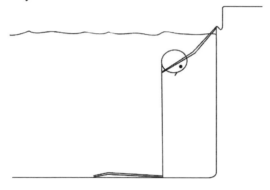

This person is probably a sinker.

For a very, very few people, the float will not work: the student will sink. You may believe that you're "a sinker." Most likely, you're not. We'll talk about sinking in a moment.

WHY SOME PEOPLE FLOAT HORIZONTALLY AND OTHERS DON'T

The position that you float in is determined by your body composition. Any parts of your body that are lighter than water (less dense) will float. Any parts that are heavier than water (more dense) will sink. The two things in our bodies that are lighter than water are air and fat. The two things in our bodies are heavier than water are muscle and bone. If you have a lot of air in your lungs, you'll be more buoyant than if you have just a little.

If you have much fat relative to your total body weight, the overall effect will be that you float horizontally. If you have less fat, you'll float less horizontally. If you have a lot of muscle and bone relative to your total body weight, your legs will sink toward the bottom (or all the way to the bottom in shallow water), or your body will sink. This is not an emergency.

The water is one place where those extra desserts can come in handy.

THREE NORMAL, GOOD FLOATS

Which one is yours?

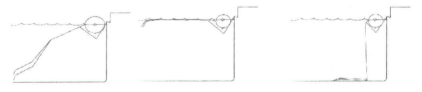

Each of these floats is perfectly good
Yours may be somewhere in between. It, too, will be perfectly good.

YOU DON'T HAVE TO BE A HORIZONTAL FLOATER
OR A FLOATER AT ALL TO BE A GOOD SWIMMER

When you hold onto the wall and put your face in the water, do you kick your feet up in the belief that they are supposed to float and that you're supposed to be horizontal? This has become a habit of many people who have tried to learn to float before. However, it's wasted energy to kick the feet up, as they will either sink on their own or they will float on their own. Your effort will not help you find your natural float. Your natural float, the effortless float, is a perfectly good float and the correct one for you. It will be different from the next person's. When you hold onto the wall, put your face in the water, and hold your breath, let yourself dangle in the water and see how the water holds you. Don't let go of the wall. Your hands' purpose will be to keep you from drifting away from the wall, not to hold you up. Let the water hold you up if you can trust it. This is how you feel yourself float, perhaps for the first time.

IF YOU WANT TO GET TECHNICAL

When you walk or do things on land, your body moves around a point called your center of gravity. You remain in balance. When you move in water, you body moves around a point called your center of buoyancy. There is such a thing as balance in the water, too.

When your center of gravity and your center of buoyancy are vertically aligned, you reach your natural, effortless floating position. If they're the same point, you float horizontally.

If you experiment with taking a bigger breath, your floating position will change. Why? Right, because you will have caused your center of buoyancy to move toward your head. If you experiment with putting your arms or feet in different places while you float, your floating position changes, too. Why? Because your center of gravity changes when you redistribute your weight.

WHAT I MEAN WHEN I SAY, "DON'T LET GO OF THE WALL"

When I say don't let go of the wall, I mean keep your fingers around the gutter and hold it with absolutely no intention of letting go, even partially.

Sometimes people think I mean, "see how little you can hold onto the wall," or, "slip your fingers away little by little so you can see how little can be touching the wall while you still feel safe." I don't mean this. If you did this, your attention would be on your fingers and how much of them is touching the wall. Your attention could not be on the feeling the float: therefore you would not be able to feel your buoyancy. Hold onto the wall in such a way that you have it and will keep it.

Let's say you're at the wall and you're thinking that the water might hold you up. You're ready to let go for a moment: you want to test it. You raise your hands off the gutter and poise them above it, ready to grasp the wall "in case something happens." When you raise your hands out of the water, they are no longer floating: they're in the air. If they're in the air, the weight of them will push you down a little bit, depending on how far out of the water they are. If they're a few inches out, you'll feel the weight push you down. If you put them higher up, you'll sink lower. When you feel yourself sinking a little bit, you may have the thought that by letting go of the wall, you sink. This is not true.

In fact, if you left your hands on the gutter or wall and then slid them into the water, you'd remain floating at the same level you were at when you were holding on. You'd find that the water holds you up even when you let go. You would not want to try this if you might leave your body, however.

Sometimes when I watch someone let go of the wall this way, her hands are shaking. This is not a sign of joy. Shaking hands mean fear. The student has made letting go of the wall her goal, rather than staying comfortable.

If your hands are shaking, you have so much fear that:

- your focus is no longer in your body: it's at the wall or at the bottom. This means *you* are at the wall or at the bottom.

- you think you have to try to float *before* you know that the water is doing the work. This is not a good idea. It pushes you to the second or third circle. This prevents you from feeling the water hold you up. *It's essential to feel what the water does for you.* If your hands are shaking, you surely are not in the first circle. Please slow down. Feel the float until you *know* the water is holding you—at least your upper body—up.

On the other hand, if you're so curious about letting go of the wall that it would be more comfortable to try it than not to, lifting your hands above the wall won't cause your hands to shake: you'll be in your body. Go ahead.

KIDDIE POOLS

The ideal place to learn to float on your own is in a very shallow pool such as a kiddie pool (a pool that's six to twenty-four inches deep), or on wide, shallow steps. You'll probably learn the float more quickly here than in a deeper pool. Only use the steps when there aren't many people entering and exiting the pool. Place your hands on the bottom of the pool or on a shallow step. Hold your breath and lower yourself down into the water. Let your feet be on the floor. If they float up, fine. Leave your hands on the bottom. Come up for air and rest anytime.

Learning at shallow steps. She can feel the water hold her up.

As you feel the support of the water, let yourself feel what's happening to your body and *in* your body. Does the water support you? How do you feel? Are you quiet inside? If not, go shallower.

105

BECOMING FREE OF THE BOTTOM IN THE KIDDIE POOL

Let yourself feel as much as you can. Make it fun and easy. Eventually, if you feel the water is doing all the work, you can let your hands off the bottom an inch, keeping them where they feel safe. This will teach you to float. If you feel wobbly, flip ahead to the section, Feeling Wobbly.

Practice feeling the water hold you up. Become convinced that it holds you. You don't have to hold yourself up. Let the water do *everything*. Can you do anything to make the water *not* hold you? Try it, if you feel confident. Can you sink to the bottom in a foot of water? I challenge you to sink!

STEP 34: BECOMING FREE OF THE SIDE IN A REGULAR-DEPTH POOL: UNFLOATING

Give yourself days of practice feeling the water hold you up and getting used to the feeling of weightlessness. Unless you've been in space, this will be new. Don't even think about becoming free of the side until you are perfectly happy feeling yourself floating at the wall, completely in control.

Becoming free of the wall means you need to know how to stand up from a float. This is called unfloating.* If you're learning in water that's deeper than a kiddie pool or if the pool doesn't have shallow steps, then move to an area in the pool where you can put your hands around one rail or rung of a ladder. If there's no ladder, we'll cover that situation in a moment.

Hold onto the ladder below the surface and float. If you know the water is holding you up—rather than your hands or feet—you can move your clasped hands behind the ladder so you won't float away, but you can feel the water doing all the work. This gives you the experience of being held up solely by the water.

Unfloat is a wonderful word created by student, Lynne

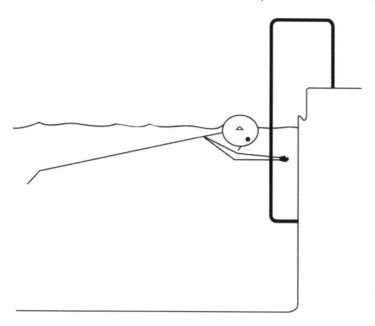

Clasp your hands behind the ladder so you won't float away,
but you feel the water doing all the work of holding you up.
Your floating position may differ from this one.

THE RICHNESS OF EXPLORATION

My favorite way for a student to learn to stand up from a float at the wall is for him to be so in-his-body that the way to stand up simply comes to him. If you eliminate causes to worry and you explore and practice while you're calm, you can't help but learn on your own.

Answers just come to you when you're fully present, at ease and in your body. By finding the solution yourself, you get "two for the price of one:" the skill plus the self-confidence that even in the water, you can discover the answers by just being yourself. This is pure gold. Proving it to yourself is one of the best lessons there is. I encourage you to learn as much as you can by exploration.

Melon Dash

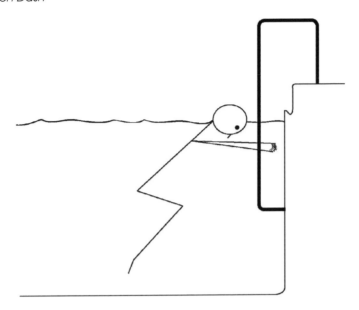

To unfloat, use your abdominal muscles
to pull your knees under you.

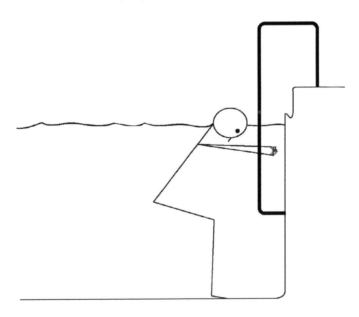

The unfloat, completed, using the ladder as security to
keep you from drifting away from the side.

As you become comfortable letting the water hold you up, in other words, when you *know* that it's the water holding you up and it's not your hands, the wall, or your feet, then you may be ready to notice other things. Do you know where your head is? Do you know where your limbs are relative to the surface? To the bottom?

Check to see if you're working. Why work? If you're not comfortable, you must have skipped a step and you need to go back to one that feels safe, one that allows you to be present.

If you'd like the steps of unfloating, here is a sequence to follow:

1. Feel the water hold you up as you hold the wall or ladder.

2. Become convinced that water does all the work.

3. Remain in your body on purpose.

4. Remain in your body while you slowly bring your knees to your chest.

5. With your knees close to your chest, extend your feet forward and below your face and place them on the floor directly beneath your face.

6. Do this unfloat while holding the wall or ladder but remain in control without using it for support. Repeat this many times.

7. When you can remain in your body for it, let go of the wall, or unclasp your hands from behind the ladder, remaining in control (in your body) and unfloating. Repeat this until you've embodied it.

8. Unfloat away from the wall or floor, remaining in control.

Spend lots of time holding onto the wall, feeling the water hold you up. What is a lot of time? It's an hour. It's 4 hours. It's 20 minutes. It's so much time that you receive all the certainty in the world that you're being held up by the water and nothing else. Why stop before you're absolutely certain? You may now have realized that letting the water hold you up and floating are the same thing.

Go slowly. We don't care if you unfloat. We only care that you feel comfortable.

If pulling your knees under you using your abdominals doesn't quite do the trick, add a downward push with your hands on the wall. Later, you can push downward on the water and you'll receive the same effect. The water is thick and dense compared to air: you can push on it.

When you know you can be at ease letting go of the wall, unfloating will come naturally.

STEP 35: THE FRONT FLOAT AWAY FROM THE WALL

When you are comfortable letting go of the wall and drifting away a bit, or even beginning your front float in the middle of the pool, let yourself dangle in your float for a while. Notice that don't have to hold yourself up. You're letting the water do *everything,* right? When you do, you will find your natural float. This position is your unique position in the water based on your body composition: your aquatic signature, as it's called by Bill Boomer, stroke scientist extraordinaire.

One difference between floating at the wall and floating in the middle of the pool is that when you're away from the wall your hands won't float out in front of you: your arms will dangle wherever gravity takes them. The other difference is that if you're away from the wall, you need enough infrastructure to stay in your body. I'm sure you know this: don't float in the middle of the pool unless you know you can stay in your body floating *and* unfloating in the middle.

When you can float away from the wall, your front float may look like this:

Front float, at ease. Notice how relaxed her head, back and arms look.
Is that you? You don't have to hold your knees straight
or your ankles bent like this, though. That's work.

UNFLOATING WHILE AWAY FROM THE WALL

When you're front-floating some distance from the wall, you can use your abdominal muscles to draw your knees under you and place your feet on the bottom of the pool directly under your face. You may have already done this at the wall.

As you draw your knees under you, you may also use your hands to help you unfloat. With your hands dangling naturally, lift them gently toward the surface so that they're out in front of you. With your flat palms and the undersides of your arms, push downward on the water. This, along with using your abdominals will bring your knees up and forward so you can then place your feet on the bottom. Remain in control and quiet inside. Once your feet are on the bottom, you're ready to lift your head out of the water.

When you can unfloat in the middle of the pool, you will have reached a milestone. It means freedom from the wall. When you reach this point, know that a world of your beginning-swimming comrades stands to applaud you.

GIVE YOURSELF A STANDING OVATION

No kidding. You've experienced a truth about water that you've always wanted to know. The water holds you up (unless you're one of the few who sink) and you are in control enough to stand up when you want to.

TRAP

If, while you're practicing a front float, you're thinking, "I wonder if this will work in the deep end," you're falling into a trap. Your body is in the shallow end, but *you're in the deep end.*

If you're in the deep end while your body is in the shallow end, you're out of your body. Therefore, your practice in the shallow will not be fruitful. You won't be able to feel every aspect of the float, for example, that the water is holding you up, or that you have tension in your limbs or neck, or that you have X amount of air, etc. You won't notice what's happening. What's more, you'll miss the realization that by doing nothing the water supports you. If unfloating doesn't work well, or if you're in a hurry while you do it, check to see if you're in the deep end while your body is in the shallow.

$$2+2=4$$

YOU HAVE TO BE IN YOUR BODY
TO KNOW WHAT YOU'RE FEELING.

Once you can feel all that the water is doing for you, you can notice what, if anything, is left for you to do.

FEELING AS THOUGH YOU'LL FLIP OVER

Sometimes as people go into their front float the first few times, they have the sensation that they will flip all the way over, as in a somersault.

You may or may not believe it, but it's absolutely impossible for you to flip over, head over heels. Many students say that when they begin to feel their feet rising up behind them, it feels as though the feet will just continue to rise. But they can't rise above the water's surface. And there's nothing to make your head go down. The buoyancy of your head is more powerful than gravity's force on it.

I am not asking you to bite off more than you can chew with this feeling of flipping. If you feel as though you may flip over, you'll need to control your float. Hold onto something. When your feet begin to float to the surface, tense your body and only allow them to float up partway. Keep them at a level where you can remain in your body. If at any point, it starts to feel scary, come up. Go slowly. Remember:

> ## WE DON'T CARE IF YOU FLOAT
> ## WE ONLY CARE THAT YOU REMAIN IN CONTROL

Take time to experience the water holding you up, mid pool. Give yourself days to practice this.

> *I have to say that when I finally felt the water support me and I could let go, I felt an extraordinary ease traveling through the water. I realized how inefficient it was for me to have expended so much energy and worry, keeping myself above water...when the water can do that for me. Slowing down and trusting the water to support me was counterintuitive for me.*
>
> —Melonie

FEELING WOBBLY

If you're floating and you feel wobbly, it's probably because you're holding your head up too high. Can you feel your neck working? The more you allow yourself to be supported by the water, the more stable you'll be.

I don't mean you have to stick your head down further into the water than it naturally goes when you rest it. If the wobbly feeling doesn't disappear when you let your head rest in the water, then you're probably holding your feet or hands up. These can make you wobble, too.

Can you feel your muscles trying to hold you up? If so, allow yourself to feel all the work you're doing. When you allow yourself to do all that work, you're likely to have the thought, "Maybe I don't have to do this." When you stop working, the wobbling will stop.

BEING A SINKER

Are you a true sinker? In shoulder-deep water, if you take a maximum breath, hold onto the wall and dangle in the water, and if you find yourself with your head below the surface and your knees parked on the bottom in 4 or 5 feet of water (5 feet, if you're tall) you're probably a sinker. A sinker is a person who, when he fills his lungs maximally and then lies down on the water, goes to the bottom and doesn't float back up so that at least the back of his head is at the surface. Try it again with the biggest breath you can hold. If you drop to the bottom, you are a sinker.

Congratulations! Being a sinker is being one of the few. You might look upon sinking with a sinking feeling. You're entitled to this but it's not necessary. Virtually every male swimmer on every Olympic swim team in the world is a sinker. And they're good swimmers, aren't they? Are they confident and comfortable in deep water? Of course. Furthermore, every male Olympic *athlete* and all the women marathon runners, sprinters, pentathletes and others with very lean bodies are likely sinkers as well. There's no reason for this to be an emergency. It's possible for you to sink and sit on the bottom, smiling. You simply need to be in your body when you sink.

Just because you sink does not mean that you won't be able to keep yourself at the surface when you want to, in any position that anyone else can float in. You'll just need to learn how it's done. While swimming, you'll stay afloat with the speed you derive from propelling yourself: you won't have to do extra work to stay afloat.

I'm not saying you have to swim fast to stay up: you don't. When you stop swimming, you'll need to apply just a little effort, doing something efficient. But the effort requires no inner hurry.

If you're a sinker, take time to practice what naturally happens when you give your body over to the combined effects of water and gravity. Take a big breath. In shallow water, drop forward onto the surface. Let yourself keep dropping down to the bottom and then kneel, sit or lie there. Is it okay with you to park on the bottom? After you've done that a few times, you may want to try turning onto your side as though you were watching TV on your bed, head propped up on hand.

All he needs is a TV.

If you either hold your nose or wear a nose clip you can also lie on your back. This is something very, very few people can do or have ever done. Count yourself among the elite.

Are you getting any sense of how important it is, and what a difference it makes to be in control? If, as you read, you're following the steps of each lesson but you're not making *staying in control* and *staying in your body* the first priority, then you're missing the message. The message is that you can't learn to swim unless you're in control in water.

> ONCE YOU'RE IN CONTROL YOU CAN
> LEARN TO SWIM IN THE SHALLOW AND DEEP

STEP 36: PRACTICE WHILE YOU'RE CALM.

Be gentle and kind to yourself. You're doing a good job of learning, of making the proper thing your first priority (staying in control). Are you seeing things in a new light? You aren't going too slowly, even if you think you are.

Give yourself plenty of time. Stay true to yourself and don't allow yourself to hurry. Getting the basics down now will make a huge difference to you later. It pays to go slowly. If you unfloat in a hurry, you may find yourself standing up with only one foot on the ground, or falling forward and having to regain your balance. Do it more slowly next time. Stay in control.

Unfloating is not important: control is. This is the purpose of unfloating with the rail or wall there. Start with lots of air and going *slowly*. You want to learn control: so practice control.

Practice the unfloat (or anything) 40 or 50 times. It's not the number of repetitions that counts: it's your full presence that counts. Practice as long as you're having fun, until you have it down. There won't be any question in your mind when you've got it. If there's a question, you don't.

Catching yourself
As you learn to stay in your body, first you learn to catch yourself.
Then you learn to prevent yourself from leaving altogether.

STEP 37: REVIEW

Over the course of your practice, it pays to do the following each time:

- Hold onto the wall

- Take a breath

- Let your body dangle in the water with no support from your hands or arms even though you're holding on

- Feel the water hold you up by itself

- When you have the thoughts, "My hands aren't holding me up. My feet aren't holding me up. The water is. Maybe I don't need my hands on the wall anymore,"

- you'll probably let your hands come off the wall. Then, when you're ready, unfloat.

If you know you'll be safe, you'll be able to let go of the wall without leaving the first circle: preliminary mission accomplished.

STEP 38: WHICH WAY IS THE RIGHT WAY?

Often students say, "Did I do it right?" And I say, "Did you accomplish your goal?" If they say, "Yes," then they did it right. Doing a skill is not about doing it right or wrong: it's about whether it works or not. At this tender stage of learning, if it's comfortable, it's right. If it makes you happy, it's right. If it functions, the form is good enough for now.

If a skill stops working—that is, if you notice something is missing that you didn't notice before—it will no longer feel right. It may have felt good before only in comparison to how bad the previous attempts felt! When you find a way that doesn't work, you'll make a new goal. Reaching that goal will improve your skill further. That becomes the new "right."

STEP 39: FEELING THE WATER HOLD YOU UP ON YOUR BACK

Ideally, you'll have shallow water—two feet or less—to learn the back float in. If not, you can use any pool that has gutters or a lip to hold onto. First we'll go through the steps of having two feet or less water. If you don't have water this shallow to learn in, skip down to the next step, Learning the Back Float at the Wall.

Sit down on the pool floor in very shallow water. One or two feet of depth will work. The more buoyant you are, the shallower it should be, down to about 8 inches. Place your hands a little bit behind you on the bottom.

Sit down in very shallow water with your hands behind you.

Let your feet remain on the bottom. (Remember, this is okay, and works better than trying to hold them up.) Lie back until your head and ears are in the water.

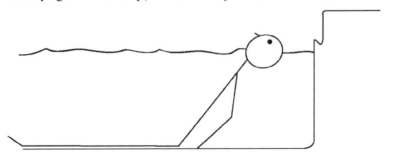

Lie back until your head and ears are in the water.

118

Take a breath and hold it. If you feel safe, let yourself be supported by the water alone, even though your hands are on the bottom.

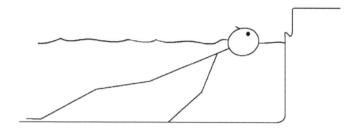

Beginning a back float in very shallow water:
let your hands stay on the bottom.

Learning the back float in very shallow water: wide steps.

Then, if you feel safe, allow your hands to barely rise off the bottom and let yourself continue to be held by the water. Floating means letting the water hold you up with no movement on your part. Spend *lots* of time feeling the water hold you up on your back.

V Float

If you find your seat dropping or your face sinking below the surface, you may notice that you're trying to hold your feet off the bottom. This will not work. If your feet seem to want to stay on the bottom despite you, let them stay. If they float by themselves, let them. Don't try to hold them up. You may be a person who floats with his feet on the bottom, especially in water this shallow.

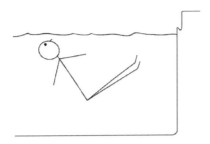 

V Float

Not to be mimicked. The V float results from trying to hold your feet up.
Your belief pulls you under: "I should be horizontal to float correctly,
so I must hold my feet off the bottom."

TROUBLESHOOTING A V FLOAT

When you lie back to float on your back, go ahead and let yourself lift your feet off the bottom again on purpose. In other words, let yourself do the very thing that pulls you under, the thing that doesn't work. You may as well let yourself do it, because you were not in control of *doing it* before, and it's likely that you are not in control of *not* doing it now. (This is not meant to be a challenge. I could be wrong if you've changed something.)

If your nose is going under water, use a nose clip or hold your nose. By consciously letting yourself do that which comes naturally—i.e. the V float, even though it isn't the original plan—and doing it several times, you'll begin to get some control over it. You'll find out how you were lifting your feet, causing your face to go under and causing your hips to drop. You'll find out how you were causing yourself to "sink." When you discover that, you'll have control over it. You'll be able to stop doing it and your float will work.

> # 2+2=4
> ## TO GET CONTROL OVER SOMETHING THAT ISN'T WORKING,
> ## DO IT INCORRECTLY ON PURPOSE

Now he's got it. No more V float.

Now, I presume that you're floating comfortably. After you have lain on your back in a float for a few seconds, you may wish to start breathing. You'll notice the effect that your breathing has on your position. When you breathe out, you drop down. If you breathe out too much, you'll sink below the surface. You'll probably put your hands on the bottom before this happens. When you breathe in, you rise up. The amount of air you have, as mentioned earlier, affects your position.

To remain afloat, most people need to keep a certain amount of air in their lungs and not exhale more than that amount. This doesn't mean you have to hold your breath: you just can't let *all* of it out. Find how shallowly or deeply you need to breathe in order to maintain the proper buoyancy to stay afloat.

Some very buoyant people can exhale all their air and still remain afloat. Many people wish they were buoyant enough to do this. Some people have to hold a maximal breath in order to float. These are the near-sinkers. Some people sink even if they hold the maximum possible amount of air in their lungs. These are the sinkers. We'll address this situation again later.

Once you feel calm and in control in your back float, experiment with the position of your hands relative to your shoulders. When lying on your back in a float, you can put your hands wherever they feel most comfortable. NOTE: if you take your hands out of the water, the weight of them above the surface will push you under water. They cannot float if they're in the air.

Experiment with putting your hands straight out to the sides at 3:00 and 9:00, as you picture a clock: your head is at 12:00 and your feet are at 6:00. How does your body position change, if at all?

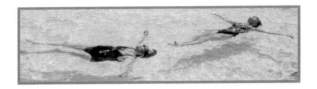

Buoyancy and back floating in two feet of water.

STEP 40: LEARNING THE BACK FLOAT AT THE WALL

If you're using a pool that has less than two feet of water, flip back a few pages to the section on learning in very shallow water. If you're using a pool that does not have such shallow water, but has a gutter or edge you can hold onto, you can learn the back float at the wall. Don't try to learn the back float without holding onto something—the wall, a ladder, or the bottom of the pool—unless you can stay in your body for it.

- In 4-5 feet of water, face the wall and hold the gutter/wall with both hands.

- Place your body flush against the wall so that your chest, stomach and thighs are all touching the wall. Your hands will be supporting your weight and your knees will be bent, the tops of your feet resting on the bottom (see below).

- Lower yourself so that your chin is almost resting in the water. Don't support yourself with your feet on the bottom: support yourself with your hands.

Following are the steps of the back float at the wall.

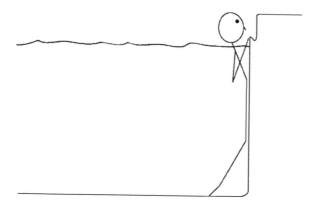

Whole front surface except shins touching wall

Then, this:

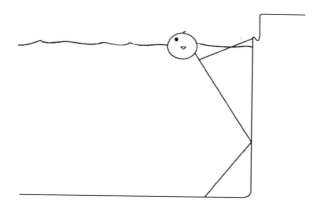

Lie back as though your head were on your pillow.
The cover of this book shows this.

Not this:

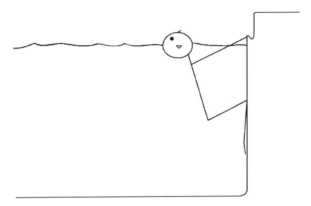

Slowly lie back in the water by extending your arms. Let your ears go into the water and let your head rest in the water as though it were on your pillow. Your head will be away from the wall a foot or two, and your hands will still be on the wall. Don't let go of the wall.

In this position, get the feeling of lying back on the water as though it were a mattress.

Then, notice whether it's your hands holding you up, your feet holding you up, or the water holding you up.

Are you comfortable putting your ears in? If not, go back to the section on making it comfortable. We (you and I) don't want you to be uncomfortable at any time. *The object is to remain in the first circle at all times.*

See if you can allow yourself to be supported by the water alone. Let the water do all the work. Your hands will still be holding the wall to prevent you from floating away. But they won't be supporting your weight.

Take a breath and hold it.

What happens? Can you feel your body rise? If you can't feel the water holding you up, take a bigger breath and hold it when you lie down on the water. You won't be letting go of the wall at any time, so you don't have to worry. Make sure you're not holding yourself out of the water with your arms.

Most students can feel the water holding them up. If you don't, make sure you have the correct body position at the wall. (See diagrams above, "This" and "Not this.")

Come to know the feeling of being supported by the water, with no effort on your part. Give yourself time to find comfort and certainty. If you can't feel the water holding you up, and you're in the correct position, then it's possible that your body is too dense to float. If you have a lot of muscle and bone relative to your total body weight, you may be denser than water and be a sinker. You're still a born swimmer. Remember what we said about Olympians. Later we'll address how to stay afloat if you're a sinker.

TROUBLESHOOTING A BACK FLOAT AT THE WALL

If you don't stay afloat on your back, add one detail: take the biggest breath you possibly can. Hold it until you're ready to unfloat. Using a nose clip helps you feel safe.

STEP 41: UNFLOATING FROM A BACK FLOAT

While you're holding onto the wall, you can come back upright (unfloat) easily just by pulling yourself up. When you've convinced yourself that the water holds you up, there comes a time when you're likely to be curious about letting go of the wall. Remember, it's more important to remain in control than it is to let go of the wall. If you know you can remain in control if you float freely away from the wall, go ahead.

If you're not sure you can remain in control, don't let go. If you did, you'd be practicing being outside the first circle.

If you know you can remain in control if you let go of the wall, go into your back float at the wall. When you feel safe, that is, when you know the water is holding you up and that you can remain in control, let go of the wall and allow yourself to drift a foot or two away. To unfloat, take a breath and curl up, pulling your forehead and your knees together. By pulling your knees toward your head, your body will automatically rotate forward into a position where you can simply put your feet down on the bottom. It may seem counter-intuitive to pull your feet up to put them down, but this is the way it works. It works easily. The key to this is to do it slowly keeping yourself in the first circle. You have enough air.

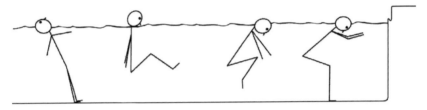

Steps to unfloat from a back float. If you're a horizontal floater, imagine the figure on the far left being horizontal.

If you wish, you may also push on the water with your flat palms and forearms as your arms come forward, giving you a little more speed.

Give yourself permission to put your face below the surface for a couple of seconds while your body is rotating into position to put your feet down. Is it okay for your face to go in? If not, then return to the section on putting your face in. You would not want to skip this step or to force your face to do something that you don't like. This would put you in the second or third circle. Stay in the first circle *all the time.*

If you're not sure you can remain in control if you let go of the wall for a back float, move over to a ladder. If someone wishes to use the ladder to enter or exit the pool at any point, he has the right of way, of course. Stand so that your side is close to the ladder. Lie back in a back float with one hand on the rail of the ladder and the other hand free. The hand on the ladder should be holding on below the surface. This way, your hand will be closer to its natural floating position.

See if you can feel the water holding you up. See if you can feel it holding you up with your hand behind the ladder, but touching it. The ladder is there if you want it.

Then see if you can unfloat without holding onto the ladder, but with the security of knowing the ladder is there. If there is any tension in your body, slow down. Feel the back float. If it makes you nervous to let go of the ladder, you're in the second circle. Perhaps you haven't convinced yourself yet that the water is doing all the work. Return to that.

Practice the unfloat until you own it. As you know, this is another big milestone that frees you. Give yourself *weeks* of practice to learn it. It may not take that long, but give yourself that long.

TRYING TO GET YOUR FEET OFF THE BOTTOM

When I say, "It's okay to let your feet stay on the bottom," students often don't believe me. They have a deep belief that floating means that their feet will be off the bottom. They think that if their feet are on the bottom in the shallow end, they'll also be on the bottom in the deep end. This would put them under water in the deep end.

The photo below shows what actually happens: the student, who floats with her feet on the bottom in shallow water, floats very well in the deep end. Her feet hang down, but they don't reach the bottom. The buoyancy of her upper body is enough for her whole body to float.

Students ask, "Shouldn't I practice floating with my feet off the bottom in shallow water so that when I get to the deep I'll be able to do it correctly?" *No.* When you're in shallow water find your natural float in shallow water. When you're in deep water find your natural float in deep water. If you're thinking about deep water while you're in shallow water, your body is in shallow water and *you're* in deep water. You won't learn the back float. You won't be able to feel it.

If your feet sink in shallow water, then in deep water, you'll probably look like this:

The back float in deep water for someone whose feet don't float
A perfectly good back float

Another pitfall of trying too hard in a back float is ending up in the V float that we discussed earlier. If you try to kick both your feet up, you'll most likely end up in a V float again. Your head may or may not go under water. Usually a student aborts his float before his head goes under.

Do you ever find yourself doing this?:

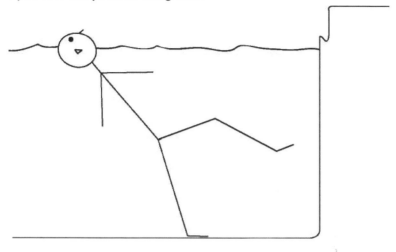

Trying to lift one foot off the bottom.

What would happen if you allowed your feet to stay on the bottom and let the water do all the work?

If you allow your feet to drop, they may park on the bottom, like this. If you kick them up, they'll end up like this every time...back on the bottom. This is a perfectly good back float.

You'd feel an easy back float for the first time. If your feet are meant to float up, they will, on their own. Otherwise, they'll stay down where they belong for your body type.

Trap

Remember not to fall into this trap: "My body is in the shallow end, but *I'm* in the deep end."

Arm Positions In the Back Float

I recommend wearing a nose clip for this next lesson. Experiment with having your hands at 10:00 and 2:00. Then try 11:00 and 1:00. Do you notice how your floating position changes? You're feeling the seesaw effect of redistributing your weight so that your body levels off: with your arms overhead at 12:00, more weight is at your upper end.

Arms at 10:00 and 2:00

Arms at 6:00

What happens if you put your hands at 12:00 (without letting them come out of the water)?

Arms at 12:00: notice how she became more horizontal
compared to the previous photo.

NOTE: some people don't have enough flexibility in their shoulders to put their arms at 12:00 without having their hands come out of the water. Remember, if your hands come out of the water, you're likely to go under. If you can't put your arms comfortably at 12:00, put them as close to 12:00 as you can, to float most horizontally.

You can also experiment with arm positions in your front float. When you float on your front, where do your arms naturally go (if your nose feels safe), without effort? Most people think they're supposed to hold their arms straight out front to do a float correctly. (That type of float is more like a *prone* float.) However, a front float is a state of being held up with no effort on your part: don't hold your hands out straight. If you let your arms (and legs) go where gravity—and buoyancy—take them, you'll find your natural front float.

STEP 42: EXPERIMENT WITH YOUR BACK FLOAT AFTER YOU OWN IT

2+2=4

WATER IS A DIFFERENT ENVIRONMENT. YOU CAN'T LEARN TO SWIM AS THOUGH IT WEREN'T THERE. YOU NEED TO RELATE TO IT WITH YOUR BODY.

Did you try it? What happened?

Can you play in your back float? If so, play with the position of your limbs one at a time and see how your balance changes. Use a nose clip. What makes you roll over onto your front? What makes you go under? What makes you stay on your back? What makes you float higher? Is there anything you can do to sink (go to the bottom) on purpose? I doubt it!

REVIEW

Many people float with their feet on the bottom in the shallow end. Why fight it? If they were in deep water, their feet wouldn't reach the bottom. But in the shallow end, their feet drop down to the bottom because their legs are denser than the water. It's okay. They don't want to waste their energy trying to keep their feet off the bottom when the water keeps their bodies afloat all by itself. Why would you?

PRACTICE

Over a few days, spend time floating on your back. Just lie there, as though you were on your bed.

Then, dangle on your stomach, hanging in the water like a wet noodle. In both floats, let gravity have your limbs and head. See what it feels like to do absolutely nothing except hold a comfortable breath. If breathing on your back float is comfortable, do that.

You need to be at ease doing nothing before you can be at ease doing something. Play with doing nothing.

FIVE GOOD BACK FLOATS

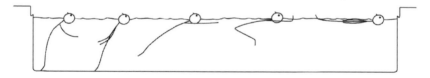

Each of these floats is perfectly good. There's nothing missing from any of them. There are many more good back floats, too.

Each of the floats above is perfectly good. The fourth floater has her wrists cocked. Her float would be fine, too, if she didn't cock her wrists. She cocked her wrists to make her hands vertical which makes them rise above the surface. This puts downward force at the upper end of her body, causing her legs to come up so she floats more horizontally. She also tucked her feet under her to bring more of her weight toward the center of her body. Not that you should or must float horizontally. This is simply an option to experiment with, to find out how things work.

STEP 43: GAMES AND TOYS

Games and toys are fun experiences we contrive in the water to learn how water works. A toy in this case is a movement you can play with.

SITTING ON THE BOTTOM

See if you can sit on the bottom of the pool in water that's 3-5 feet deep. Only do this if it sounds like fun, of course. The game is to park your suit on the bottom of the pool (without taking your suit off). Bouncing off the bottom is an intermediate step toward the parking, but it's not the goal. See if you can sit down and stay for 3-4 seconds.

Parked, and proud

Sitting on the bottom takes more know-how than you may have thought. How can the student above sit on the bottom and not panic? He has learned to remain in control. He knows he's safe. There was a time when sitting on the bottom of a pool was the last thing on his agenda. He may have thought it was a crazy idea at first but he was curious. Since he wanted to get there, he was in his body—he could receive signals his body was giving him and he could keep himself safe. Eventually he figured out how to remain in complete control and to sink on purpose. Now he can't think of a reason to panic.

What would it take for you to lose your buoyancy and sink? The process of learning to *swim* should include learning how hard it is to sink. Learning to sink teaches you how the water and your body work together. It's a worthwhile game.

If you can sit on the bottom, you may want to try lying down on your front on the bottom.

A novel feeling

We talked about this earlier in relation to being a sinker. It's a good game.

Lying on your back on the bottom is novel, too. As previously mentioned, use a nose clip or hold your nose. The goal is not really to sit or lie down on the bottom: it's to find out how hard it is to get there. It's to understand that in order to sink, you really need to know how to do it. If you don't know how, you won't sink, as long as you remain present. The only way a person can sink if they

135

are normally buoyant is if they panic and exhaust themselves by thrashing and giving up all their air.

When you have an experience that takes your body to a new "place," you can expect that in the next few days you'll have a brand new thought. It may not have anything to do with swimming. But because you went into new territory with a new physical experience, you can expect to go into new territory mentally soon after.

BECOMING A BALL

After you feel quite confident in your front float, draw yourself from a front float into a smaller package. Contract your body so that you're no longer a body-length long, but a foot shorter, pulling your knees toward your head. As you know, we don't care if you move in the direction of making a ball: we *only* care that you feel in control as you move.

Front float away from wall:

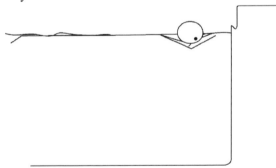

When you've been in this new position for a while, contract a little more. Pull your arms and feet closer together so that you're nearer to the shape of a ball. Again, we don't care if you move in the direction of making a ball: we only care that you feel in control as you go.

Making your body into a smaller package on your way to becoming a ball

If, as you move toward being in a ball you start to leave the first circle, go back to a more extended position where you can return to the first circle. Wait in this position until your body gives you signals that it's safe to proceed.

If you're in control and it sounds like fun, pull yourself fully into a ball, with your arms wrapped around your knees.

The ball

Notice how your balance changes just a little bit when you're in a ball. Stand up whenever you want.

Go back into the ball and rest there. Get to know "ball." You can't hang suspended like this on land. Enjoy it.

Why is this important to swimming? Because it teaches you something about your balance in water. Because it helps you to understand how your body and the water work together. Because you're practicing being present (in control). Because it brings your awareness and presence to a new position. Because each new position you reach teaches you that you can do one more thing in water that makes you that much more free. If you're like my students, you want to be able to play.

BOUNCING BALL

If there's a friend in the pool with you, you can take turns being a ball or being a bouncer. When you're the ball, your friend can place his hands on your back and gently push you toward the bottom. It should be a gentle push so that you don't reach the bottom with your knees or feet. Then, just wait. In 3-4 seconds, your body will stop going toward the bottom (at the effect of his push) and will start to float back up at the effect of your buoyancy.

You'll bob back up to the surface. Your balance will change a bit. Then, if you have plenty of air and you stay in the ball position, your friend can push you back down again. It's just another playful thing you can do in water that you can't do on land and which teaches you how the water reliably pushes you back up.

When Joan was the ball (and was having a ball), her knees grazed the bottom from this slightly too enthusiastic push.

SMILING UNDER WATER

Go under water and see if you can smile. You could smile a toothy smile, or a closed-mouth smile. When you feel safe, you'll find the toothy smile rewarding.

Next, try coughing under water. Then pretend you're sneezing. Naturally, you would only do the exhaling part of both coughing and sneezing. You can also swallow under water with your mouth closed. It's good to know that if you need to do any of these things, you can be safe for them.

DANGLE

Hang in a front float. Imagine that you can attach a Relaxation Meter to your entire body. On a scale from 1-100, what would it read (100, being totally limp)? If it doesn't read 100, dangle again. Feel your shoulders, back, neck, arms, legs, abdomen, jaw, ankles, fingers. Feel any tension that's there and let it be there without trying to change it. What does your body do when you don't resist how you feel? When you're 100% calm?

PERMISSION TO USE NOSE CLIPS

From this point forward, if you haven't already agreed to one, I highly recommend that you have a nose clip. Though you can learn to prevent water from going into your nose as we discussed before, or you can hold your nose, if you have not mastered keeping water out of your nose yet and you try a new skill without a nose clip, you'll be splitting your attention between the new skill and keeping water out of your nose. This, we have established, doesn't work.

Resist any temptation to think you "should" know how to keep water out of your nose. Let yourself be where you are. This helps you to come back to your body where you can learn.

The next lesson is one that will require that you protect your nose. Therefore, please get a nose clip if you haven't already.

PHOTOS IN THE MIDST OF LEARNING

Here are a few photos of students who had taken most of the steps in this book: they started from where you are now, or close.

You learn so well when you're having fun.
But first, you need to feel safe. These people learned to feel safe.

Picture yourself having fun in the pool. What would your photo look like?

We stopped to witness the miracle of classmates floating freely and joyfully for the first time after years or even decades of terror in the water. For most of us, whether we were young adults, middle-aged, or elderly, it was the first time we experienced childlike glee and freedom in the water.

When every cell of our being was finally convinced the water would hold us up, we floated and paddled around in the deep end of the pool. And when it happened, it felt miraculous and completely natural and thrilling and transformational. And we did it without learning the crawl stroke, the flutter kick or the butterfly. We did it by going slowly, step by step, until we internalized confidence and trust in the water. Not one of us believed Melon in the beginning when she said each of us was born a swimmer the same way she was born a swimmer. Now we knew it was true.

-Tut, "A Novel Approach to Healing Fear of the Water"

STEP 44: LEARN STEERING

Each time you get into the water, start from the beginning. Review the basics and become quiet inside.

In the water, when you're ready, go back into a ball. Then, let go of your knees with one hand. How does your balance feel? If you're okay, use the flat palm of one hand to push on the water so that you turn sideways 360 degrees (a complete circle, called "a 360"). Maybe you have enough air to turn around in circles several times. When you've figured out how to turn a 360, turn yourself the other direction using the same hand.

Turn clockwise. If you push left on the water, you'll move to the right.

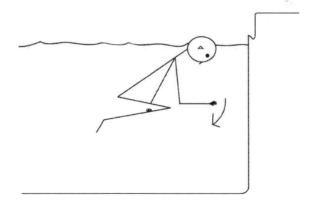

Turn counterclockwise. If you push
right on the water, you'll move to the left.

Then, use your other hand and turn a 360. When you're familiar with the way that feels, use that same hand to turn a 360 in the other direction. Then, use both hands to turn a 360. How can you use your hands in such a way that they *both* help you turn in the direction you want to go? Play. Putter. Goof around.

STEP 45: FIND HAND POSITIONS THAT WORK

Go into your ball again and turn yourself in a 360. This time, experiment with different hand positions. First, turn a 360 with your fist clenched (just one hand). Notice the purchase (grip, traction, amount of pressure) you get on the water with your hand in a fist. Notice the efficiency of turning a 360 with your fist. How well does it propel you, relative to the effort you use?

Next, do a 360 with your hand open, fingers splayed. How does this feel compared to the efficiency of your fist?

Fingers splayed

Next, do a 360 with your hand cupped.

Hand cupped. How does this efficiency compare?

Next, do a 360 with your hand horizontal, so you push on the water with the edge of your hand. The edge of your hand and your pinky will be pushing on the water. How well does this work?

When you're rested, try a 360 with your hand flat, like a pancake, so you're pushing with your whole palm and the face of your fingers, which are together. It's okay if your thumb is away from your palm. To have it touching your palm takes more effort than it's worth.

Both hands are flat as a pancake. "Pancake hands:" good position.
Both the palms and the backs of your hands are as flat as a pancake.

How well does this hand position work compared to the others? Swimming students have been told for decades that the correct hand position for maximum efficiency is cupped. Perhaps you could tell that other positions allowed you to move more effectively through your 360. If so, you know that cupped hands are *not* efficient. You might have intuited that cupped hands were not correct, as it's too much work. If something is a lot of work in the water, chances are good that it's not correct. In other words, it doesn't work well compared to something else. Keep that in mind.

Other hand positions also demand too much work for the same amount of movement. Therefore, they are not used in swimming. The most efficient position, and perhaps you found it for yourself, is the last one: flat as a pancake.

STEP 46: FEEL, DON'T THINK

While you're learning, it's fine to focus on the most workable hand position. But focus on the *feeling* of it. Look at your hand and feel what works best for you. Do it over and over until it becomes second nature. Don't try to add to this skill until you have embodied it.

Why *feel* instead of think? Because when you feel, you bring your presence to the feeling and in this case, to your hand. Your body gives you feedback to let you know what's happening. You will recognize an efficient position as opposed to an inefficient one.

You also would want to feel instead of thinking because you don't want to try to remember how to hold your hand at the same time that you try to remember the step that builds on hand position. You can't have your attention in two places at once. If you try, you're not fully present to either one. Therefore, you can't learn either one.

Sometimes I see someone swimming with his hands in a strange position. I know that he didn't learn by feeling. He was trying too hard when his hand position was "learned." He never would have said, "This feels right." As a result, he didn't learn the efficient way. He is now swimming slower and working harder than necessary.

Be completely in your body for the one thing you're doing. Practice it until it comes naturally. When you can do it "on automatic," you've mastered it enough to do it without being fully present. When you've mastered it enough to do it without being fully present, you'll have attention to spare for learning something else. Only then is it time to learn something new.

I know you know this. But how often in our lives do we ignore this truth and try to cram more into our time than it's possible to absorb? It doesn't work. Give yourself the best chance to succeed by setting up the situation to work every time. Give yourself time to play and absorb each lesson: be in your body.

What Is Swimming, to You?

What does swimming mean to you? Does it mean doing the freestyle, fast and pretty? Is it getting from here to there, no matter how uncomfortable it feels? Or, is it moving easily and confidently from here to there without regard to depth?

As mentioned earlier, I define swimming this way: confidence in water. Once you're confident in water, you'll automatically be able to move from here to there in water (swim) with comfort, control, and ease. Once you're confident in deep water, you'll be able to move from here to there in deep water with comfort, control, and ease. Strokes are learned *after* swimming is learned.

Ease

What is it that makes you feel at ease in the water?

For most people, it's having enough air and knowing they can remain in control and get air or stop to rest when they want to. Anyone who's worried about sinking is only worried because he isn't in control of coming back up for air. Is this true for you? Ease comes from knowing you're in control and you're safe.

> *From time to time I find myself sinking without planning to. It's usually when I'm in the deep end under water watching students. It happens because I took a smaller breath than I needed in order to stay in place. It's a humorous moment when I find myself not staying at the level where I'd planned to be. But why worry? I'm in control. By pushing down on the water, I'll come right back up. –Melon*

STEP 47: PROPULSION: YOUR FIRST SWIMMING

Ease is the operative word, whether you're swimming in the shallow or deep. Hopefully, you wouldn't "put yourself out" (to the second or third circle) to swim. Your goal is to be in your body.

If you haven't moved from here to there in the water yet with ease, try this in shallow water. Lying in a front float, hang there listlessly. Feel how the water holds you up. You don't have to hold yourself up, right? The water does all the work. You're not kicking your feet off the bottom, are you? If you're kicking your feet off the bottom, you haven't learned the front float yet and it's *not* time to swim. Be kind to yourself and return to the section on front float.

If you want to move from here to there, you don't have to do anything to stay up: you only have to do something to take yourself over there.

PRONE FLOAT

Stretch your body out into a long streamlined position called a prone float, arms at 12 o'clock and feet at 6 o'clock:

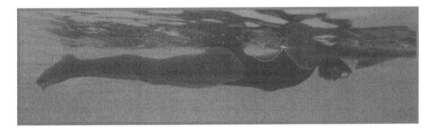

The streamlined position of a prone float. This student becomes horizontal in a prone float. If you're not buoyant and your feet are at the bottom of the pool, that's okay as long as your body makes a straight line from toes to fingertips.

Spend a few minutes in this position. You'll be looking at the bottom of the pool, not forward. Get your balance. Your balance in this position is different than in a front float.

Recall the front float, which is different: you don't hold yourself in a straight line—you just dangle limply.

TIPPING

If you feel yourself tipping, you can stabilize yourself. One way to stabilize is to make sure you're not holding your head up. Another is to spread your hands apart. If you need more stability you can spread your feet apart as well. Experiment. Once you stabilize, move your feet closer together (so your legs are parallel). If you feel stable in this position, see if you can slowly move your hands back together so your arms are parallel. If you still tip quite a bit, you're probably stiff, or holding your head up, rather than being at ease. If you don't like feeling tippy, and you can't stop it, it's not time yet to do a prone float. See what allows you to do a front float comfortably. Take your time. When it's time, your curiosity will lead you back to a prone float again. You don't have to do a perfectly balanced prone float to be ready for the arm pull, which is next.

ARM PULL

Now your body is in an efficient position (prone float) to move through the water. Pull your flat pancake hands backward to your thighs. Do this by pressing on the water with the palms of your hands and the entire inside surface of your arms. In other words, form the largest surface area you can with your hands and arms in order to push on the greatest area of water. Flat hands create the largest surface.

This is the correct hand position for stroking.
He pulls himself through the water efficiently.

After you've swept your hands and arms back to your thighs, let yourself glide through the water as far as your sweep takes you. Why not get all the distance from it that's possible? That way it takes fewer strokes to go from here to there, and it therefore uses less energy. Most people can glide longer than they think they can. Spend time at the end of your arm sweep, hands at your sides, just gliding.

Sweeping his arms back to his thighs, he propels himself...

through the hoop.

After your arm sweep, when your forward motion dies down, bring your hands back to the front, creating the smallest amount of resistance possible. Draw them from your sides together under your belly, one atop the other. With the palms of your hands almost touching your belly, slide your hands up your torso, the thumbs and edges of your hands slicing through the water, all the way up until your hands are out in front of you again. Turn your hands over as you reach forward at the end of this recovery (recovery is the return to the beginning of the arm sweep). Recovering efficiently prevents you from creating excess drag.

When your hands are out in front of you again, take another arm sweep back to your sides with your "pancake" palms and inner arms. Feel the pressure on the flat palms of your hands all the way through your sweep. Your *palms are the most important part* of your body in propelling you through the water. Put your attention in your (pancake) palms. By taking strokes, you'll go from here to there. Let your legs trail quietly.

TRAP

When you begin to swim from here to there, you may be tempted to see if you can swim *all the way* across, or to see *how far* you can go. This is the "get to the side rather than enjoy the trip" trap. If you're focused on getting to a certain point, *you'll be* at that point, and your body will be back where it is. But remember, the goal is for you to stay where your body is.

Start swimming again, but this time, and forevermore, be where your body is while you propel yourself. Feel the sweep with your palms. Feel yourself moving through the water. Watch the bottom go by. Feel the glide. Feel your air supply. By being in your body, you'll know what to do in each moment to keep yourself comfortable. Your body will tell you, and you'll be there to hear it. Congratulations for understanding this distinction and using it.

You are entering swimmerhood.

The Most Important Factors in Learning to Swim

What are the most important things to learn about swimming? Would you say, "Not drowning"? "Getting to the other side"? "Being able to breathe"? "Staying up"?

I believe the most important things to learn about are these, in this order:

Control

Breath

Balance

Hands

We've already established that without control, you have nothing else going for you: you can't get anything else to work. Control is the number one priority. Once you're in control, you can enjoy yourself and have fun.

Breath is obviously a big priority. You won't be able to do anything with your breath however, unless you're in control. Once you know how much air you have, how much air you need, and when it's time to get more, it frees you to play in the water. You can play for as long as you can hold your breath. This ushers you into a new world if you haven't played in water before. There are many things you can do in water that you can't do on land. To be able to hold your breath and be a kid in the water, finding out how your body and the water work together is to start to understand the water. A nose clip can aid you immensely. In time, you'll learn to get air whenever you want it, with ease.

Balance is your stability. When you're in balance, you can be in a position without falling out of it. If you're in balance you feel that you're not in your own way.

Your hands are the action part of swimming and propulsion. Specifically, your palms (pancake palms) are your link to moving through the water. It's here that you connect with water to propel yourself. Yes, your feet do some of the work, but it's your hands that do the lion's share of connecting and propelling.

The connection of your hands to the water is a matter of your presence to what your palms feel. If you become very sensitive to your palms, you can learn the best path for your hands to take through the water when you take a stroke. Without thinking and totally by feeling, your hands will find still water to press upon. The more still water (as opposed to turbulent water) your palms press upon, the more propulsion you'll get from one sweep of your arms.

From time to time, you see a swimmer who needs fewer strokes than anyone else to swim down the pool. Their stroke rate is slower than everyone else's yet they're going faster. These are the people who have a fabulous feel for the water. They have tremendous presence in their hands. Their hands naturally find the best path through their stroke, and they use less energy to swim.

IMPISH TEMPTATION

Let's say you're able to swim a few strokes across the pool with the arm sweep and glide. As you swim along and it's working well, you have the thought, "Okay, I can do this. Now, how can I take a breath?" You start trying to get a breath.

This is an impish thought. Why? Because it's very likely that if you've only swum a few strokes across the pool a few times, you are not 100% in your body yet. You aren't 100% in control of yourself. But the temptation to try the next step is often great. To ask yourself to be in control of getting a breath at this point is *not reasonable*.

How *does* it work, then? In order to get a breath, you must not be attached to whether or not you get one. But the impish thought is likely to be rife with attachment: "If I could *only* get a breath!"

If you try to learn to breathe at this point in the game, it is likely to place you "on hold" (stuck, contracted about breathing) for weeks, months or even years. I don't want to put any limitations on you, but it's highly unlikely that it's time for you to try to get a breath right now (except if you stand up to get one). I urge you not to. Spend more time just pulling and gliding, feeling everything and enjoying it.

Instead of trying to get a breath, go back a step. Spend more time—lots more time—swimming along with your arm sweeps, gliding, learning. Learn about your glide time. Learn about your balance and how it shifts. Learn where your feet are throughout your glide. Learn about the position of your hands as you sweep. How few strokes can you use to go a certain distance? What position is your head in? What are you looking at? Are you 100% in your body and having fun?

You must be completely in control before you can learn to swim. You must be completely in control swimming before you can learn to breathe while swimming.

When you go "backward" to become more comfortable with the basic

Going Backward Is Going Forward

Jerry came to class to learn to breathe. He did not believe that he was afraid in water. He had taken swimming lessons and he had many swimming skills, but he had not been able to learn to breathe while he swam. When he went to deep water, he had to hold onto the side. Being in the middle of the deep was not an option. Still, he said he was not afraid and that he just needed to learn to breathe.

When it came time in class to learn about breathing, Jerry followed the steps one by one. He "could do" the step that comes before adding breathing to the swimming, but he couldn't do it comfortably. Still, he was convinced that he was ready to add the breathing to the swimming.

He practiced swimming and trying to get a breath. He practiced for a few hours and became very frustrated. He didn't make a shred of progress, in his own mind.

I suggested that he go back and embody the step that came before putting breathing and swimming together. I told him I could see that he was able to perform it, but he hadn't mastered it: he wasn't at home with it: he was slightly ahead of himself. He politely obliged me, but he seemed to be resisting. Since he didn't feel that this was the way he should be using his time, he resumed trying to breathe while swimming. He could not be led to the idea that he had not yet embodied Step 1 and that he had to embody Step 1 before he went to Step 2.

He is still struggling with the breathing, three years later. This is what going at his own pace requires in this case. Since he could not be convinced that to succeed he must go back, he will have to learn this truth on his own.

skills, you're doing the one essential thing—dropping further down into your body—that will prepare you for what comes next in your learning sequence. So going backward really is taking you a step closer to your goals. Going backward is going forward.

**BY BEING IN YOUR BODY LONG ENOUGH
YOU INEVITABLY COME TO A BREAKTHROUGH**

Many people believe that in order to swim, they simply need to learn to breathe, tread water, or move their arms correctly. But no matter how many swimming classes they take, they cannot swim.

Remember, the goal is comfort, not skill at this point in your learning. In the water, being in control is part of comfort. If you are not successful learning a skill, there's something missing: you're not in control. Control needs to be brought to light and harnessed in order to learn. This is true of learning anything.

You won't learn the mechanics of breathing if you're afraid you won't get enough air. You won't learn to breathe if you must get to the other side, or you think the water might not hold you up, or that you might "lose it." And you won't learn to swim if you're afraid of looking silly, or if you feel you must learn today in order to get your money's worth or because you're going on vacation or you've just entered a triathlon. You must be in your body to learn.

**SLOWING DOWN MAY APPEAR TO BE THE WORST POSSIBLE
STEP. BUT *NOT* SLOWING DOWN CAN CAUSE WORSE AND
PROLONGED PAIN.**

GAME: TIPPING AND ROLLING

This is a skill that's done best with a nose clip for now. If you feel comfortable in the prone float, and if it sounds like fun, see what happens when you take a breath and go into a prone float and then tip sideways on purpose. Can you find a way to make yourself tip? It doesn't require thought. Just feel.

2+2=4

ALWAYS TAKE A BREATH BEFORE YOU
PRACTICE A SKILL IN THE WATER

To tip on purpose, you can turn your head one way or the other. Or, you can place one arm across your body. See what it takes to put yourself out of balance and let yourself roll. You may end up on your side, your back, or on your front. See where your balance takes you.

Rolling over

When you take time to play with balance, it helps you understand how your body works in the water. You'll find out, among other things, that the water holds you up no matter what creative position you get into. This is good to know!

SEAL ROLLS

Seals roll over like hotdogs on a rotisserie (but faster). Lying in a front float, do something that will take you off balance. Go slowly and make being in control—not rolling over—your goal. Use a nose clip.

Going slowly, now see if you can roll yourself all the way over from your front to your back, and around again to your front, like a seal. It doesn't matter if you do it—or how you do it. It only matters that you stay in your body: that you feel in control.

> **IT'S MORE IMPORTANT TO REMAIN IN CONTROL THAN IT IS TO DO A SEAL ROLL**

Use your hands, that is, your "propellers" to keep rolling until you have turned 360 degrees, as though you were on a rotisserie. If at any moment you feel as though you're about to do something uncomfortable, *stop*. Give yourself a moment to gather yourself, and stand up.

SWIMMING BACKWARD

From a front float, see if you can propel yourself in the direction of your feet. If your body doesn't remain in the same floating position, it's okay: your feet may drop. This toy teaches you more about propulsion.

STEP 48: BACK FLOAT PRACTICE

Spend more time in your back float. Practice getting into it, coming out of it, and the different things that come up when you do a back float. What happens when you breathe deeply? You'll want to try this with a nose clip on. Review what happens when you take a deep breath and hold it.

What happens when you let a lot of air out? What happens when you take shallow breaths, but get enough air to feel comfortable?

Notice whether you're allowing your feet to go where they naturally go. Do you try to lift them off the bottom? (Since I can't see you, I have to pose this question from time to time.)

Notice whether your body feels loose as you float on your back. Is there any tension? If so, where is it? Remember to allow it to be there. Only when you allow it to be there can you return to your body. Then tension can melt away. It will, if you allow it long enough.

STEP 49: LEARNING TIME

Now and then, students get impatient with their progress. They want to know everything yesterday. They want to take a pill and learn how to be free in deep water in a minute while still on land. How are you doing with your patience? How long should it take to overcome fear of water? To learn to swim? What are your expectations?

Write your expectations here:

1. _____
2. _____
3. _____
4. _____

Although it's not *probable* that your fear will be completely healed today or tomorrow, we must hold that anything is possible. And it is.

However, the beliefs you have concerning yourself in water and in deep water had time to grow roots. When you pull weeds out of the ground (this is not to say that fear is a weed), you're careful to pull them out by the roots so they won't grow back. We do the same thing with your beliefs.

Give yourself time for the roots to loosen and pull free.

You can think of overcoming your fear of water in the same way. For example, you wouldn't want to force your face into the water when you really don't like having your face in, and then swim across the pool feeling tense and uncomfortable.

If you do something you don't like—such as putting your face in the water—and try to build a new skill on top of it, you divide yourself in two. You cannot be 100% present to the new skill, so you cannot learn it. Presumably you want to get to the root of the discomfort and change it to ease and comfort. *Then* you can swim across the pool, enjoying every moment.

The amount of time it will take you to overcome your fear in water is the amount of time it takes to let go of old beliefs that aren't true about the water or yourself, and to learn to trust yourself in water. This is neither difficult nor mysterious.

> WHEN YOU'VE BROUGHT YOUR AWARENESS ABOUT A SKILL OR BELIEF COMPLETELY INTO YOUR BODY, YOU'VE LEARNED IT

You'll accomplish both letting go of old beliefs and trusting yourself in the shallow and deep by learning how to remain in your body, letting yourself be where you are, and just *feeling* it. All the healing you seek will take place from there. When you're *out* of the pool, you can examine your beliefs as the root of discomfort in the water. Your beliefs determine how your body will feel when you're in the water.

When you're *in* the pool, where feeling the water is obvious and present, the starting point for learning is the way you *feel*. You can feel your beliefs. Or better said, you can feel the effect of your beliefs. Your body is your feelings-gauge. It's also your beliefs-gauge. Your body gives you signals just like a traffic light does: *Stop. Go. Caution.*

When you're in the water, watch for your body's signals. When it signals caution, slow down and stop. When it signals stop, *stop!* Don't run a red light. In fact, don't run a yellow light. If you do, you're putting yourself at risk of panicking. Once you're in the second or third circle, it's easier to fly out to the fifth circle than it is if you're in the first circle and focused on staying there. Keep yourself in the first circle.

Don't run a red light.
Don't run a yellow light, either.

Step 50: Make the Second Circle Your Red Light

He ran a yellow light.
He left the first circle.

He regrouped.

As soon as you feel yourself outside of the first circle, *stop*. Stop and regroup. Get back in the first circle where you're in control and where you can learn.

How long will it take you to learn to swim the way you dream you can? It's different for everyone. It partially depends on how much you let things happen rather than pushing them. Are you willing to try the lessons and ideas in this book? I hope so. It will pay off, and sooner than you may have thought possible.

If you would be comfortable going to the pool to practice once a week, give yourself 6 months to a year to learn the teachings and skills in this book. It would be fruitless to hurry. This is a reasonable amount of time for this course, doing it on your own. You may learn sooner or it could take longer. If you follow the steps, and skip none, you cannot miss. That's a promise.

STEP 51: PUSHING YOURSELF—MORE ON "GOING BACKWARD IS GOING FORWARD"

If you've been practicing something for days and nothing seems to be happening, check that you're practicing while you're in your body. If you don't seem to be making any progress, you're probably:

- pushing yourself (and therefore out of the first circle),

- practicing something that's too advanced and therefore you're tense and out of the first circle,

- skipping a step which would put you out of the first circle, or

- in the future or the past which are also out of the first circle.

These all boil down to one thing: pushing yourself.

You cannot learn a skill when you're in the past, in the future, or you're pushing yourself. If you perform a skill once or twice, that's all well and good for the moment, but it will not "stick." You'll have to return to it and become present to it if you want to learn.

Go "backward." You're trying to go from Topeka to Denver before you've gone from Atlanta to Topeka. Go back to a step of the same skill that was completely comfortable.

Spend more time with that step and get to know it better. Do it until you can practically do it in your sleep.

$2+2=4$

IT'S MORE ADVANCED ON THE "LEARNING METER" TO BE COMFORTABLE AND *NOT* COMPLETE A SKILL THAN TO COMPLETE IT AND BE UNCOMFORTABLE

STEP 52: THE LEARNING METER

The Learning Meter measures how much learning is taking place when you go to the pool. When you practice, where are you on the Learning Meter?

Low   Medium   High   Mastery

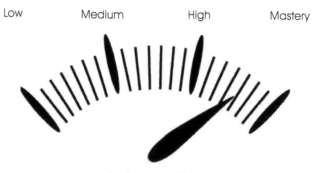

The Learning Meter

Measures how much learning is taking place.
Your level of learning (1-4 below) varies with your presence.

1	2	3	4
• Low quality of instructions	• Medium quality of instructions	• High quality of instructions	• Mastery: "Got it"
• Poor level of learning	• Moderate level of learning	• Good level of learning	• Learning level has become "owning"
• Not fun	• Hopeful	• Fun	• You feel oneness with yourself and the water. Fun
• What am I doing here?	• I'm getting somewhere.	• I'm learning and healing.	• I have "arrived."
		• More, please.	

to

to

This figure is explained in the section on Mastery

Quality of instruction is a measure of how well the instructions match your need. Are you met at your level? Is your question heard and is it answered?

Level of learning is the progress you make due to an answer you're given. Information that's understood can be used fruitfully.

Learning doesn't always mean you're doing something new: it can also mean that you're continuing to embody something you started practicing earlier.

STEP 53: LEARNING PATH

We think of the learning path as being a straight line.

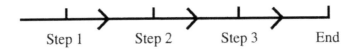

Step 1   Step 2   Step 3   End

But I am sure you have experienced it differently if you've been reading this book and practicing in the pool. At times, one skill leads directly into another but sometimes you may find yourself taking side trips—or doubling back.

A normal and perfectly good learning path can look like this:

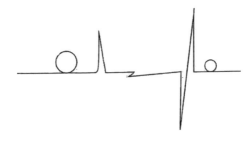

The shape of a perfectly good and normal learning path.

For instance, you may be trying to float on your stomach at the wall. You discover that you've been kicking your feet up, trying to keep them off the bottom. This is uncomfortable, so you take a side trip to examine why you're uncomfortable. You learn that you're not supposed to kick your feet up; they go where they're supposed to go by themselves, and you don't have to help. You realize that your belief about your floating position needed to change. It changed.

Or, in the middle of learning to turn over onto your back, you may find that you haven't yet learned how to keep water out of your nose. So, you take a side trip to learn about nose clips or about keeping water out of your nose. When you get that down pat, turning over becomes a cinch.

Sometimes you do something new that's far ahead of anything you've done before. You wonder how you got there. You hope it will happen again. You're excited and you wonder what is next. You start looking for your next leap. It's probably not time for the next leap. It's probably time to fill in the space between the leap you just took and where you leapt from. It's time to fill in the gap.

Fill the gap with awareness. Find out what you did. Embody the skill you just performed so you can do it at will. To try to go to the next step would be to build on a shaky foundation. If you wish to continue such leaps, spend a lot of time embodying the step you're comfortable with. Master it! How much time is a lot of time? You'll know when you've gotten it. More on this soon under, "Was It A Fluke?"

When you master Step 1, you *automatically* move to Step 2. You don't even need a teacher or a book.

When there are huge leaps followed by dropping back and filling in the space, this is good learning. There's no error or waste in any part of it.

From here,   you leap to here.

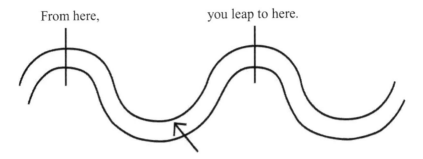

Then you go back to fill in this space.
This is not regressing.

When you climb a ladder, you advance by placing your foot on a rung and pushing yourself up. Each time you push yourself up you get closer to your goal.

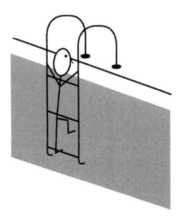

When one foot is on its way to the next rung, there's no progress *upward*. You must make this movement to make progress upward, however.

If you can't "see" your swimming progress, look a little deeper. See if there's an increase of your presence in water, causing you to be more "there," more at ease, more one with the water, more aware. This progress is what fills the space between where you are and a leap to a new place.

Spend time embodying each step of this book. At any moment, you are either on your way to the next rung, or on the next rung.

> **AT ANY MOMENT, YOU ARE EITHER ON YOUR WAY TO THE NEXT RUNG, OR ON THE NEXT RUNG.**

STEP 54: UNDERSTANDING "CAN"

"I can swim across the pool (but I can't wait to get to the other side)."
"I can put my face in the water (but I hate it)."
"I can exhale through my nose into the water (but I have to force myself.)"
Each of these skills is being accomplished with tension.

If a swimming instructor asks you if you can do X, Y, or Z, and you have performed X, Y, or Z five times in your life, the answer to the question is not necessarily, "Yes."

If you "can" do the skills, but only uncomfortably, think of it this way: you can't do them yet. You can't do them the way we (you and I) want you to. If you're uncomfortable, you won't enjoy the skills and you probably won't relish practicing them. It would be foolhardy to try to build something new on top of them. Going swimming becomes a burden.

"Can do" the skill means "doing the skill with ease." Go back and get comfortable. Start from calm. Start from comfort. Proceed *very slowly*, staying in your body. If you're proceeding slowly, then stopping the skill will also be slow and easy.

STEP 55: "PAVING NEW ROAD" EXERCISE

Make a list of the skills in which you feel *any* tension in the water. If you haven't been in the water yet, you may need to wait until later to do this.

1. _____

2. _____

3. _____

4. _____

5. _____

6. _____

Mentally review one skill at a time. Imagine doing it slowly: so slowly that you see or feel every part of it. Choose one skill and write down the sequence of steps you see in your mind's eye.

1. _____

2. _____

3. _____

4. _____

5. _____

6. _____

The first few times you imagine the skill unfolding, there may be some gaps in the "movie" in your mind. These are places where you don't know what the skill looks like. Break it down even more. The gaps may get filled in by themselves. If not, fill them in with what you would like to see there.

When you have a satisfactory movie, replay it for practice. Visualizing is practicing. Feeling is practicing, too (some people feel rather than visualize).

WAS IT A FLUKE?

Sometimes, out of the blue you do a skill correctly that you've never done before. It's a complete surprise. It feels good, it's easy, and you know you did something right.

You made a huge leap forward. You search your memory to see how you did it. You go into your head—and leave your body behind. You search for a mental map that led you "out of the blue." But the map is not in your head: it's in your body. You connected to the map with your presence. You performed a new skill by doing what was fun for you in the moment. It unfolded as you moved through it. This is what you want to repeat.

To develop a map that gives you the control you need to repeat the skill, start over from the same place with a simple plan: be present. *Let go of whether it "works" again or not.* Let the moments unfold. The breakthrough may or may not happen just as it did before. *It doesn't matter.* Be prepared to let *anything* happen. When something feels right, follow it. Only by coming upon it naturally—maybe five or ten times—will you realize what your body did. Let your body lead you. *The benefits of this cannot be overemphasized.*

When you discover what your body did, you are filling in the space mentioned above: you're building a map. When you've let your new skill unfold by itself enough times, you'll be able to do it intentionally. *Trust your body. It knows things that your mind does not.* All you need to do is to be there and let it happen. After a while, you'll be able to do the skill on purpose.

> TRUST YOUR BODY. IT KNOWS THINGS
> THAT YOUR MIND DOES NOT.

STEP 56: SWIMMING ON YOUR BACK

When you feel comfortable in your back float and you know it well, you can swim on your back. For now, this means using your arms only and letting your feet trail (just rest them). Since we can focus on only one new thing at once, we will begin with your arms. Do this activity in a part of the pool that feels completely safe so you can focus on your new movement. If you're thinking you might go into deep water, you'll be distracted. You can have total focus on your skill only if you are completely in your body.

> **MAKE SURE YOU DON'T HAVE TO FOCUS
> ON STAYING OUT OF DEEP WATER**

This is the whole arm sweep for swimming on your back. Imagine that the figures are lying on their backs in shallow water:

- Starting in your back float, slide your fingertips up your sides to your armpits.
- Send your hands straight outward to the sides so that your torso and arms form a "T."
- Sweep your arms through the water so that your hands come to rest at your sides. The palms of your "pancake" hands and the insides of your arms are the surface that pushes on the water. This will thrust you backward in the direction of your head.
- The sweep is horizontal, just below the surface. Your hands should not break the surface or cause a splash.
- Let yourself glide as far as your sweep takes you. You may as well get all the distance you can from each pull.

172

If you float horizontally in a back float, your feet will remain at the surface when you take this sweep.

If you float with your feet low or on the bottom in your back float, the thrust of your arms will cause your feet to rise up, perhaps all the way to the surface. When you lose the momentum from that arm sweep, your feet will drop back down. Let it happen. Don't worry about your legs. Be completely there for your arm sweep. There's a lot to learn from this alone. Play with it. Get to know it.

STEP 57: HOW TO KNOW WHERE YOU'RE GOING ON YOUR BACK

We don't want swimming to become a sport in which you have to wear a helmet. Open your eyes while you're on your back, if you can. When you're going somewhere on your back remember, you have a neck! You can watch where you're going by turning your head and looking to the sides. Turning your head won't upset your balance.

Using his neck, he checks his surroundings.

While you're parked in a back float, try to look all the way behind you to see a full 360 degrees. (Don't hit the wall with your nose.) Of course, you can always stand up to see where you are. When you're indoors, you can track your location by watching markings on the ceiling or wall. If you're outside, you may be able to sight on a pole, sun umbrella, rooftop, etc.

AVOIDING BUMPING INTO OTHER PEOPLE

Most likely, you don't want anyone to bump into you and you don't want to bump into anyone else. For the most part, you are in charge of this. Before you take off on your back float each time, look around in the pool. Is anyone going to reach you by the time you lie back for your float? What are the children in the pool (or standing beside it) doing? Learning how to judge this will give you a feeling of safety. When you're on your back, you can still check when necessary. If you bump into someone, the object is to *stay in your body*. You don't *have to* get flustered. Feel what's happening and let yourself handle it. The right thing will come to you, whether it's to stand up or to swim around someone.

CHANGING DIRECTION ON YOUR BACK

What do you think will happen if you sweep just one arm as you swim on your back? Try it a few times. Try it with the other arm. It will work best if your sweeps are horizontal, as mentioned before. If you sweep downward, you'll find yourself bouncing upward out of the water and then coming back down.

Practice changing direction on your back so you feel in control of where you go. Give yourself plenty of time to play with this. Let your legs just follow you around.

MORE GAMES ON YOUR BACK

There's plenty you can do to familiarize yourself with how the water works while you're on your back.

1.	From a back float, see if you can propel yourself in the direction of your feet. This may seem awkward. Its awkwardness is one reason that it's not used as a stroke. Still, it's informative— and it might make you chuckle.

2.	From a back float, see if you can roll over onto your front. It's like rolling over in bed.

Rolling from back float to front float

ROLLING OVER TO REST: FRONT TO BACK

If you knew how to be in control, and you could roll over from your front float to your back float, and you knew how to rest in a back float, you could *get air whenever you wanted it in deep water*. This next skill is a good one to practice using a nose clip until you've got it down. If you did the seal rolls above, you probably already have it.

To review, if you aren't in your body for a front or back float yet, go back to that section, as this next skill can't be learned yet.

From your happy front float, ask your body to turn over. Your body will respond well. Because you're in your body, you have control over this. You'll intuitively know how to start rolling.

> WE DON'T CARE IF YOU ROLL OVER.
> WE ONLY CARE THAT YOU REMAIN IN CONTROL.

As you begin to roll, check in with yourself. Is it okay to be on your side? If so, keep rolling. When you get to your back, put your head back enough that your face will be out of the water. Lie in your back float with your head in a comfortable position. There *is* such a thing as putting your head back too far: your eyes go under water. Just make your face and neck comfortable.

If you didn't make it all the way around, but you stayed in the first circle, *great*. If you made it all the way around, but you felt panicky, you forgot to put comfort first. Do that next time.

> **IT'S MORE ADVANCED TO REMAIN IN CONTROL AND ABORT A SKILL THAN TO LOSE CONTROL AND COMPLETE THE SKILL**

Why? Because the goal is to remain in the first circle *all the time*. This is what makes you safe. It's *this* that creates a safe swimmer.

Of course, there's an in-between stage, the stage of uncertainty that can fall between control and fear. Uncertainty, as long as you feel safe, is okay.

TRAP

If you said to yourself, "I want to learn this without my nose clip," and you took it off and proceeded to get water in your nose, you demonstrated the method to my madness: focusing on rolling over, you no longer could protect your nose. You can only be in one place: in the roll, or in your nose.

If you anticipate getting water in your nose *next time*, you'll be focused on protecting your nose and won't be able to focus on rolling over. I suggest you wear a nose clip until blipping becomes a habit.

Step 58: Coordination

What does "coordinated" mean? It means moving in an organized way. It means you and your body are synchronized. It means being in your body—you and your body moving as one. How can you become coordinated? By listening to your body.

If you're pushing yourself, you probably won't move in a coordinated way. Sometimes you're "moving" so fast you don't notice that you're out of your body. Slow down and feel what your body is doing.

Let's say you're learning the back float. You feel the water supporting you and you know you're floating. Your inquisitive self asks, "Can I swim on my back to there?" If you're in your body, swimming to there is a cinch. You feel in control. Your balance is there. You can feel the progress of each stroke. It's not tiring, and it feels coordinated. If you're not in your body, you may get there, but it won't feel good. You might notice that your stomach is tight, your neck is stiff, or your balance is off. Don't swim there on your back until you can do it under control. Come home first. Comfort allows coordination.

You can have your full attention in only one place at a time. Make sure you've mastered the back float before adding your arms. If adding your arms—even though you don't have your back float down—sounds like too much fun to pass up, then go ahead and try it. But be prepared: it's possible that you'll leave the first circle.

Remember, when one skill becomes part of you—when you embody it—you can fix your attention on something else. When you embody the second skill, the two will be coordinated. Surely you don't think you could fail at learning anything. This is a formula for success: you can learn any skill if you're present.

> ## THERE'S NO SUCH THING AS BEING IN YOUR BODY AND BEING UNCOORDINATED

STEP 59: BREATH

It's not time to learn to breathe as you swim yet, but let's get started with the elementary points.

EVERYDAY BREATHING

As you sit in your chair, there are two main parts of your breathing: inhaling and exhaling. Both take about the same amount of time. However, it takes much more time and effort to exhale into the water than it takes to exhale into air. This is because water is much denser than air. You have to push your air into the water.

On land we breathe through the nose most of the time. However, while swimming, we breathe *in* through the mouth, because its opening is relatively big, allowing inhalation to be swift. We breathe *out* through the nose because this prevents water from coming into the nose.

BREATH EXERCISES

Stand in a place in the pool where you feel completely safe and grounded. You may want to hold onto the wall with one hand for stability.

If you're not comfortable putting your face in water, go back to that section of the book and build the skill slowly. You can't fail if you go at your own pace and skip no steps. There's plenty of time.

As you stand in the pool, imagine yourself inhaling a comfortable breath and exhaling into the water through your nose or mouth. If you want to use a nose clip, you'll exhale through your mouth. Imagine that you've lowered your face into the water and you have plenty of air. Visualize blowing your air out, causing bubbles to pop up all around your face. The harder you blow, the louder and bigger the bubbles will be. The softer you blow, the quieter and smaller.

When you can see this in your mind's eye and you're ready to experiment, try these games.

Breath and Nose Toys

1. Standing with your face above the water, begin to exhale. Lower your face down to the water and, still exhaling, (preferably through the nose but if necessary through the mouth), dip your face in and bring it right back out. Keep exhaling the whole time. See if it's okay to exhale into the water for this brief amount of time. Do this a number of times until it becomes old hat.

2. Exhale short bursts of air outward into the water. Feel what part of your body stops the exhalations.

3. Exhale into the water through your mouth, with your lips pursed. Notice how long your exhalation takes. Then exhale into the water with your mouth wide open. Notice how long your exhalation takes.

4. Exhale into the water through your mouth or nose. Stop exhaling in the middle of your breath. Then resume exhaling.

5. When you come up for air, see what happens if you inhale through your nose instead of through your mouth. Anything?

6. Exhale through your nose into the water. *Let* air come out instead of pushing it out. Come up and inhale through your mouth. Repeat this as long as you're having fun.

7. Exhale through your nose into the air and feel the warmth in your nose as compared to the coolness of inhaling through your nose.

8. Take the biggest breath you can. Exhale through your nose into the water as slowly as you can.

9. Do #8 once again but this time exhale at a normal rate. Notice how long it takes to exhale to the end of a normal, comfortable exhalation.

10. Take a deep breath and hold it. Time how long you can hold it if you haven't timed this already.

11. Take a deep breath. Then exhale all your air into the air, every last wisp of air you can push out. At the very end, without inhaling, time how long you can remain at the end of your breath before you must inhale. After you've done it, notice that you're still alive.

The idea of these breathing toys is to get to know your breath capacity and gain control over your breath. Once you have control over your breath, it gives you more freedom to play in the water.

STEP 60: WATER RUNNING OFF YOUR FACE

Water running off her face

When you come up, water will run off your face. A small amount may run into your mouth as you open your mouth for a breath. Take time to feel this. It will not interfere with the inhalation of your breath. If you have a lot of hair, more water will drain off your face and into your mouth unless you tie back your hair or wear a bathing cap. The water usually ends up under your tongue, the lowest part of your mouth. Go ahead and take your next breath, then go under and expel the water from your mouth. Do this by squirting it out (not spitting). You don't even have to open your mouth. Barely parting your lips is enough. Then finish exhaling your air until your body tells you to come up.

STEP 61: BREATHING

Take a comfortable breath and exhale into the water again. When it's time to come up, do so and take a new breath. Return to exhaling into the water. To continue this for a while, you'll need to exhale the same amount that you inhale: what comes in must go out. If your air exchange is even, you'll be able to continue this indefinitely. If it's not even, you'll get winded.

As you exhale, feel the air in your lungs decreasing. Since you're in your body, your body will keep you from coming up too soon or too late.

Find a slow, comfortable, easy rhythm. It should feel easy and natural. Do we care if you inhale air and exhale it into the water? No, we don't. We only care that you feel comfortable and in control—that you're in the first circle. Agreed? See how long you can go up and down breathing this way without getting tired.

You cannot force all the air in your body out of your lungs. There will always be a residual amount of air left in your lungs that prevents them from collapsing. If you feel out of breath in the water, remember that you still have this residual air to live on. You might want to get air right away, and that's okay but it would not be time to panic yet! (You know I'm kidding, right? It's never time to panic...unless you choose it.)

181

TROUBLE-SHOOTING BREATHING

1. If you don't like exhaling through your nose, exhale through your mouth. It will work just as well in the position you're using for this exercise (head vertical or slightly forward). You can return to exhaling through your nose when you're ready.

2. Let's say you want to exhale into the water and your breath stops short: it doesn't want to come out. That's okay. Give it your full permission to stop. *Let it not come out.* Give yourself plenty of time to feel what's happening when it stops coming out. It's outside of your control for the moment, but you feel safe, so go with it.

When you've done this for a few minutes—and you feel as though you understand it—see if you can stop exhaling on purpose. Do this for a few more minutes. It's not worthwhile to force yourself to blow out the air. Forcing yourself would be putting yourself outside the first circle. That doesn't work in the long run. Practice being in the first circle *all the time.* Being in control is more important than just "getting it done."

3. If You Get Tired, Out of Breath, or Light-Headed
If your air exchange is not even, that is, if what comes in is more than what goes out, you'll become winded: out of breath. This is the most common problem for people who have learned to "swim" but who "cannot get the breathing." They don't realize how much air they must breathe out to make it work. Take more time to exhale while your face is in the water. Or, exhale faster.

If you exhale more than you inhale, you'll get lightheaded over time. Slow down and regroup. Make your air exchange even and comfortable.

It fell apart.

I regrouped.

If you still don't like putting your face in water, forget about learning the breathing for now. Go back and take the appropriate steps *from where you are now.*

The goal of this breathing exercise is to be able to exhale into the water and come up for air repeatedly, for minutes at a time, without getting tired. It becomes a rhythmic, comfortable exercise. Ideally, you'll be able to breathe out through your nose and mouth interchangeably. Eventually, you'll probably prefer to exhale through your nose exclusively since this prevents water from entering your nose.

STEP 62: CHAIR TOY

Try this new position. After taking a breath, sit on the water as though you were on a lawn chair but with your feet slightly out in front of you on the bottom.

Go into a sitting position as though you're in a chair.
Your arms may float like this, or higher. Both are okay.

Lean back just slightly. Keep your head vertical, so you won't risk getting water in your nose. Your face will be partially or fully submerged. If you find that your feet float up or your face does not submerge, raise your arms vertically overhead.

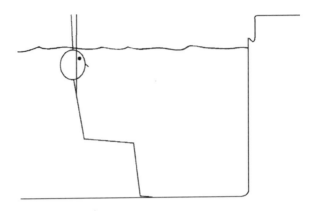

Raising your arms overhead pushes you down,
since they can't float in the air.

The weight of your arms above the surface will push your body slightly downward. This should cause your feet to reach the bottom if they hadn't already. If they're still floating, that's okay.

Take time to get your balance. Practice this chair position for a few minutes, standing up for air when you need to. Get accustomed to your balance. Become comfortable with holding your breath and coming up to rest whenever you need to. Do this until you've got it down.

Now try this. (This is a good time to use a nose clip.) Putting your hands in the water just below the surface and using your "pancake hands," (your flat palms and the whole inside surface of your arms), sweep downward on water toward the bottom and see what happens.

Ready to sweep downward with the largest surface area possible

After the downward sweep

What happened? Did you get the result you expected? If all went according to plan, you pushed yourself up and out of the water. Your chin came above the surface.

The faster you push downward, the higher up you'll go. If you push down very, very slowly, you may find no rise whatsoever. Experiment with different speeds and pressures and see their effects.

The point is to lift yourself above the surface, then to let gravity draw you back down.

NOTE: Your hands should be held in line with your forearms: pancake hands and no bending at the wrist, or you'll lose your purchase on the water. What is "purchase?" It's the hold you have on the water, or the "grip" you get on it, or the "traction" you get when you push on it.

Good hand position: keep your hand this way. Flat as a pancake
(both the back of the hand and the palm are flat).
Recall that the thumb doesn't need to be next to the forefinger.

If your hands are in any of the following positions, they will be much less effective:

Hand bent downward: you have less purchase on the water

Hands cupped: you lose more purchase on the water

Hand bent upward: you lose even more purchase on the water

When you rise above the surface as a result of your arm sweep, you stay up for a moment. Then gravity takes over and you drop back below the surface. When you go back under water, you could get water in your nose if you didn't wear a nose clip, so do. If you simply cannot find one, then go back and learn to blip.

Gravity takes you back under water as low as your buoyancy will allow. Then, buoyancy takes over and you start floating toward the surface again. Gravity. Buoyancy. Gravity. Buoyancy. These are the two natural forces we play with in the water. Did you notice this? You have to *wait* for your body to go down and come back up. When you've begun to float back up, *ask your body* when you should make your arm sweep downward. *Your body will tell you.* Practice this. It's important. When you spend time with these two natural forces, going up and down, you'll see how little effort is needed to bring yourself above the water.

If you find yourself coming up too slowly, you probably need to take a bigger breath first. If you're a sinker, you won't float back up: it may take you two or three arm strokes to come back above the surface. Whatever works is okay.

As we said earlier, two things make you float: air and fat. Remember, whenever you begin to practice something in the water, take a breath just before you go under: it gives you added buoyancy. You'll find yourself taking the breath through your mouth simply because it's quick and convenient, not because you're in a hurry.

During this exercise, you're holding your breath the whole time (if you're wearing a nose clip). Go down with gravity. Come up by using buoyancy first, *then* your arm sweep. Repeat this until it feels easy and natural. Stand up to rest when needed. Give yourself days to learn this.

When you rise toward the surface every time, you can feel that the water does most of the work. You can rely on this. Part of its reliability depends on the fact that you have air in your lungs. The more air you have, the sooner and the faster you'll come up. You add just a little effort with your arm sweep at the end of your buoyant ascent.

Experiment with different amounts of air. You don't need to come out of the water to your navel. Just come out so that your chin clears the surface.

I call this exercise "bouncing off the water." It's as though you're bouncing off an imaginary line in the water where gravity loses its pull and your buoyancy takes over (the point where you stop going down and start coming back up).

She's on her way down, then, BOING!
Bouncing off an imaginary line. Let the water do the work.

When you become comfortable with this skill, you will have learned the first steps of getting yourself into position to get air. *Do not push yourself. Don't get ahead of yourself.*

STEP 63: FALLING TOYS, WHALE JUMPS, QUARTERS

Stand with your arms at your sides in chest-deep water. If it sounds like fun, fall forward into the water keeping your body in line (straight) and see what the water does with you. It will be a very slow, gentle fall to the surface as though you're falling into Jell-O.

He was in waist-deep water for this fall.
He had already done it in chest-deep water.

Do this five or ten times. Get the feeling of falling, what to expect, and what happens after you "land." Then move to water that is 5 or 6 inches shallower. Fall into the water again with your hands at your sides. Get the feeling of falling from this "height." Learn what to expect and what happens after you "land."

Go to water that's waist-deep. Fall into the water with your hands at your sides. You won't hit the bottom or come close. Your head will most likely not even go under water. Get the feeling of falling from this "height." Learn what to expect and what happens after you "land."

Are you getting an idea of how resilient the water is? How dense a mattress it is, relative to air? How you can depend on it to catch you

189

and hold you up? Can you allow the water to have you, without any resistance on your part?

You can even go to water that is knee-deep and do the same exercise. If you keep your body straight, you'll still land on the water and your head will barely go beneath the surface if at all. Sound like fun? If not, you can work down to this depth, a few inches at a time to prove to yourself that you're safe.

FALLING SIDEWAYS TOY

In chest–deep water, practice falling sideways into the water. You may want to use a nose clip or hold your nose. See how it feels to fall sideways. See what your body does. See where you end up. Then do it in waist-deep water.

> ## DO WE CARE IF YOU FALL IN SIDEWAYS? NO.

We only care that you feel completely in control. If falling in sideways sounds like something that would cause you to lose control, then naturally you wouldn't do it—until you're ready. To make it easier to fall in sideways, you may prefer to start with your shoulders under water so you're falling from a lower point. It's more important to stay in the first circle than to fall. Don't do anything that would cause you to leave the first circle unless it sounds like fun.

Review:

Q: "But if it's not comfortable, shouldn't I practice it until it becomes comfortable?"

A: No. Remember, you're all too familiar with being uncomfortable and out of control. It has not made you happy: it has kept you from learning. Practice control. The messages of this book are so dependable that in our classes, we guarantee that people will learn to swim as long as they try the teaching. To try it is to become convinced.

WHALE JUMPS

Have you ever seen a whale breaching? It looks like this:

Two whales breaching

Using a nose clip, start with your own mini-whale jumps. If you've mastered the Falling Sideways toy, then crouch a bit and take a little jump and let yourself fall sideways. Do this for a while, becoming more and more confident (in-your-body) as you do.

Then, be like a child and do a whale jump. Crouch down in the water and launch yourself with reckless abandon out of the water sideways, backward, or forward. Let gravity take you where it will, and let buoyancy bring you back to the surface. There's no work for you to do once you've self-launched. A nose clip prevents you from having to be concerned about getting water in your nose. Or, hold your nose.

Whale jump

How can you look dignified and self-respecting doing whale jumps in a public pool? Well, you can't. But if it's okay with you, it will be okay with others. It's just fun and, it pays off. Here's Nina coming back down from a whale jump.

Coming down from a whale jump

QUARTERS TOY

Throw a quarter to the bottom of the pool.

Go get it. You'll find a way to get it, one way or another.

To make it more challenging, throw it into chest deep water.

To make it more challenging, throw more than one coin in. Count what you throw in.

To make it more challenging, throw in smaller coins that are harder to pick up.

What did you learn?

STEP 64: HOW DOES FEAR HEAL?

To become free in water, there are two things to do: conquer your fear and learn to be confident. Conquering fear deals with the past. Learning to be confident deals with the present. They can happen concurrently. In this book, we skip no steps: we do both. This section is about conquering fear. That means healing it.

These days, it seems that we handle fear in one of two ways: we avoid it or we manage it (get around it). Healing it seems to be such a mystery that few people really try. Individuals and therapeutic relationships try to heal fear. Some are successful. Institutions such as government, the media, business, and medicine don't usually try: they only hope to manage it. Swimming lessons as a whole manage it, too: "Don't be afraid," or, "Learn strokes and treading."

As far as I have seen in 35 years as a teacher, managing fear does not satisfy afraid students. Managing fear does not allow a person to be in his body, comfortable and in control. It eventually leads a student to find reasons not to go to swimming class.

The reason to avoid fear is self-evident: it feels better. But it only feels better in the short term. It doesn't help or feel better in the long run. Over time, avoiding fear is tiresome and disappointing. It can erode self-esteem. When we avoid fear, we miss the opportunity to have a successful, empowering experience—or to permanently change our lives for the better.

If everyone knew that it is safe to confront fear, that there is a step-by-step process to follow that would not be forced upon them and which they could take at their own pace, a process that's simple, easy and fun, then maybe we would all be more enthused about facing our fears. Obviously, moving from fear to confidence is extremely life-enhancing. Is there such a way for us all to *heal fear*? Yes.

HEALING FEAR IS THE WAY OUT

Healing fear is a learning process. It's simple. It can take a little while or a long while. If correct steps are followed and none are skipped, it's predictable and certain: you cannot possibly fail to overcome fear. You cannot fail any more than 2+2 can fail to equal 4. It's that reliable and simple.

HEALING FEAR IN STEPS

This section is for people who like to "dissect" things. It is very detailed. Take what you can use and leave the rest.

Think of a friend, a family member or even an acquaintance in whom you have complete trust. This is someone you trust as much as you trust yourself, holding them in the highest regard. We'll call this person Sue.

Let's say that Sue needs to borrow a car for the day and she asks if she can borrow yours. Sue borrows your car. You're very comfortable with this. You have absolutely no qualms about it. You don't give it a second thought. As it turns out, she totals your car.

Sue is a person you trust. You figure, "If Sue totaled it, chances are just as good that if I'd been in the same situation, I could have totaled it, too." You instantly and completely let Sue off the hook.

If Sue asked you the next week if she could borrow your car, you wouldn't think twice about it. You both might laugh. But you would lend her your car in a second, because you still trust her. Your trust had not diminished.

Let's say that instead of Sue asking to borrow your car the second time, Joe asked if he could borrow it. You don't know Joe that well. You're unsure, but you let him borrow it, with reservations. Joe totals the car.

If Joe asked to borrow the car again, you probably would not lend it to him. You probably don't trust Joe anymore.

What is the difference between these two scenarios? You began with a different level of trust in the two people who borrowed the car. But that is not the operative factor. The important thing here is that you forgave Sue. Therefore, you're not afraid to lend your car to Sue again. You did not forgive Joe. Therefore, you are afraid to lend it to Joe again.

By the way, when I talk about forgiving, this again has nothing to do with religion. It is about letting *yourself* and another person off the hook to *free yourself*.

When Joe totaled your car and you didn't forgive him, you set yourself up for a predictable result: a new fear would be born, the fear of lending Joe (or a stranger) your car. You didn't do this knowingly, of course. But the fear could not help but follow. Now, anytime you're asked to lend your car to Joe or to anyone you don't know well, you'll be looking back over your shoulder at what happened last time, which appears to be the last time you lent your car to a stranger, but which is really "the last time you didn't forgive someone for having an accident with your car."

195

IF YOU DON'T FORGIVE, A FEAR IS BORN

Or just as certain, an old fear will grow stronger. No fear grew from lending your car to Sue because you forgave her. Check the truth of this for yourself.

If you don't forgive yourself or someone else for whatever happened to you in the water that made you afraid—you won't become totally free in the water. You'll be "you, who made a mistake or who had a bad experience last time." You won't trust yourself. You'll look back over your shoulder to make sure the same thing won't happen again. If you're always looking back over your shoulder, you are not in the present. You cannot feel what's happening right now in the water. You can't feel all the good things that are working for you.

When you decided that you couldn't trust someone anymore because of what happened, (and that someone could be yourself) you basically said, "This felt so bad that I never want to experience it again. I will never do this again." Your intention was good: to protect yourself. But the invisible fine print that comes with this decision is, "…and I will leave my body if I ever get near this situation again. It's too painful there."

> *Fear is paralyzing, but learning to forgive my fear…had the opposite effect. I became courageous, in-control, a master of my life. After reading your book I began to think about other fears that I had, and I addressed them, one by one.*
>
> *I applied for a public service position in my small town. I started speaking in public, (so far I've talked to over 300 people this year). I taught my daughter to drive; this was really scary. I purchased several pieces of real estate. I am leaving my job of 10 years at the end of June.*
>
> *Looking at fear from your point of view has really changed my life.*
>
> *—Deborah*

> **IS IT POSSIBLE TO LET YOURSELF OFF THE HOOK FOR WHAT HAPPENED IN THE WATER (OR OUT OF IT) THAT MADE YOU AFRAID?**

If yes, you're well on your way to freedom in water. You could skip the next few pages up to Step 70. If not, or not yet, read on.

WHAT PREVENTS US FROM FORGIVING?

By not forgiving, we think we protect ourselves. We believe—before we do any forgiveness training, and without examining what we're doing—that if we forgive, we stand the chance of getting hurt again. We believe that we need to remain vigilant against the threat of this pain. This vigilance is fear.

No one does this consciously, I don't believe. It's our default mechanism until we become more aware. Who doesn't want to protect themselves from another substantial hurt?

However, it works just the opposite way. If you forgive, you protect yourself more than if you don't forgive. You protect yourself because without being afraid, you have a softer, gentler approach to life, or at least a softer, gentler approach to the water. You can be more present.

1. If you forgive, and then something new happens that demands your full attention, you'll be present for it. You'll be able to feel the signals your body is giving you to guide you because you'll be in your body. On the other hand, if you didn't forgive and you are still afraid that you might get hurt again, you'll be thinking of avoiding the same thing that happened last time, which may not actually be happening this time. You can't feel what you actually need now.

2. If you forgive, you drop a burden. Further, if you forgive, you stand a far smaller chance of being hurt long into the future by

the hurtful incident that happened. For example, if you forgive Joe's totaling your car, then you won't carry the pain of holding it against him, you won't dislike or mistrust Joe, you won't be afraid to lend your car to trustworthy people you could help, and you will then have the opportunity to be helped by them in return.

We can acknowledge this: if we forgive, there is a pain for a short while. We have to grieve what we lost in the incident. This grieving is so worthwhile that we ought to have a holiday for it, in my opinion. Letting yourself grieve the loss allows you to put the innocent error behind you. Consider this: if you don't grieve and forgive, the hurt will keep on hurting. For big hurts, this lasts decades or even a lifetime.

Something happened that made you afraid in water. Perhaps

- you were held under water by your older brother when you were both children, and you've been afraid in water ever since.

- your father threw you into a pool against your will and said, "Sink or swim! I learned this way and so can you."

- you were being carried into the waves on your mother's shoulders and she stepped into a hole and both of you fell.

- your mother was afraid in water and she told you that water is unsafe. Naturally, as a child you believed her.

- you were cultivating a tentative sense of security in water in high school but at a party your "friends" picked you up and threw you in, despite your cries that you couldn't swim.

In the first one, your brother thought it was funny to hold you under water, that you'd be okay, and he had no idea he was causing damage. In the second one, your father had good intentions: it had worked for him and he thought it would work for you. In the third one, your mother didn't know there was going to be a loss of control. In the fourth, your mother thought she was protecting you and herself. In the fifth, your friends were under the influence of each other's egging-on and may have known they were in the wrong. But they couldn't stop themselves.

In each of these scenarios, an innocent error was made. It was a purely innocent error, one made by you and perhaps one made by someone else. It's possible that an error was not innocent if made by someone else—but it probably was. Errors are innocent because they are caused by not knowing. Even if someone should have known better, they made the error because they let something overtake their better judgment. They didn't think about the consequences. That was their error. Let's figure out what the error was and take the steps to forgive it. If a fear was born, an error was not forgiven.

Perhaps you're saying, "I don't feel comfortable with the idea that I made an error. It just happened to me. I was an innocent bystander." If this is the case, please look closely. Something happened. You didn't know how to handle it. You handled it in a way that didn't work for you in the long run. That was the "error." It was such a purely innocent error that I have given it a name: *inno*. An inno is a purely innocent error you made that came from not knowing. Remove all the negative charge from "error" and you have "inno."

Look back to see when your fear in water began. What happened? What did you lose? If you can't remember how you became afraid, ask yourself where your beliefs about water came from. Finding out where you got your beliefs is a step toward healing.

Was there a situation you couldn't get out of? Was there a moment when you lost control? Was there a moment when you believed (perhaps not consciously) that you *had* to leave your body in order to get away from the pain? It may have been the single smartest thing you could have done at the time, but until now, you never looked at it this way. Was there a decision you made that you *never* wanted to repeat an experience again, thereby limiting yourself in ways you couldn't know at the time?

What happened: _____

_____

_____

_____

_____

_____

What did I lose? _____

Forgiving *yourself* is a requirement for healing fear. There are no exceptions, as far as I have seen in my career. You may need to forgive another person as well. This need not be a chore.

You may have thought that being held under water caused you to be afraid. Or that being thrown into a pool made you afraid. But these were just the circumstances, not the cause.

In all situations that I have heard so far,

> FEAR CAME WHEN YOU INNOCENTLY LEFT YOUR BODY TO AVOID PAIN, AND THEN DIDN'T FORGIVE YOURSELF FOR LEAVING

If you abandoned your body automatically, even instinctively in order to avoid pain, and you did not understand *why* you did it, you probably didn't forgive yourself. Forgiving yourself may have never entered your mind as a necessity. That's understandable. Who knew they left their body? Who knew it was important? Then, a new fear was born, or an old one grew.

Whatever happened that made you afraid, and there are many more stories than the ones above, there are ten common denominators among all of the fear-producing incidents I have observed:

1. There was a very painful experience.

2. The person decided he didn't want to experience that pain ever again.

3. He didn't know that by deciding not to experience that pain again he would have to leave his body to prevent experiencing/feeling it if the situation arose again.

4. The situation arose again.

5. He left his body, just as he had unknowingly decided to do.

6. By leaving his body he lost control of himself. He lost control of what his body did.

7. He interpreted his loss of control as his being non-trustworthy to take care of himself in that situation. He stopped trusting himself in that situation.

8. He became afraid and decided to stay away from that situation altogether.

9. He hasn't forgiven himself for leaving his body.

10. He wishes he knew how to get over his fear.

Now, consider these:

- Do you agree that you believed that something was going to feel so bad you didn't want to experience it? Yes _____ No_____

- Do you agree that you made a decision, consciously or not, to leave your body if that situation arose? Yes _____ No_____

- Do you agree that you left your body next time the situation arose in the (unknown) belief that it was the best thing to do at the time? Yes _____ No _____

- Do you feel that it was an inno to leave your body to protect yourself from pain? Yes _____ No _____

- Do you agree that you left your body not knowing that if you remained in it, you'd have more control? Yes _____ No _____

- Do you agree that you didn't forgive yourself for leaving? Yes _____ No _____

- Do you agree that you made a decision to no longer trust yourself in that situation as a result of what happened? Yes _____ No _____

- Are you ready to re-examine your decision? It doesn't matter whether you make the same decision again or not—as long as you stay true to yourself. Yes _____ No _____ Maybe_____

If you want to forgive, or if you're not sure, then first identify the inno.

The inno(s) I made was: _____

_____

It was innocent because: _____

_____

The inno someone else made was: _____

_____

Their inno was innocent because: _____

_____

The decision I made as a result of the episode/accident was: _____

_____

Try not to get bogged down with these forgiveness steps.

WHAT DOES IT MEAN TO LOSE CONTROL?

When we're in the first circle, we're in our bodies. We're in control of what we do. When we leave our bodies—even a little bit—we begin to lose control. In the second circle, we still have some control. In the third circle, we have very little control: we're losing it. In the fourth circle we have virtually no control and in the fifth circle, we've "lost it:" lost all control.

Once you know that you can stay in your body to prevent the loss of control, you have a power that children don't have. Usually, we do what's needed in order to survive and to avoid pain. But there is more power available to us if we want to have it.

You and I don't ever *lose* control. We give it up. We let ourselves leave the first circle. *This is good news.* It means that we *can* be in charge of our experience once we learn how to remain in control. It may feel as though we lose control, but that's only because we didn't know we had the power to keep it.

LOSING CONTROL IS ACTUALLY GIVING UP CONTROL

We may have known we had the power to keep it but we hadn't made it our Number 1 priority yet. Once we learn that it's up to us, and that keeping it is a choice, we can keep it on purpose. We get better and better at this with practice.

Keeping it means staying in our bodies. Out of control is out of your body. Staying in our bodies requires going slowly and continuing to *feel*. Control is a location.

Sometimes we are so in the habit of giving control away that it takes a lot of focus to "stay here." And sometimes it's so scary to stay here that we can do it only if we know that someone else will keep us safe. In our swim school, this person is called a spotter.

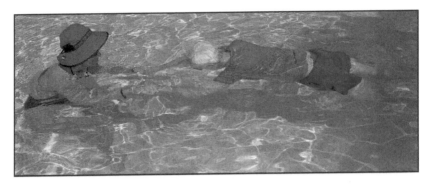

On the left: a spotter, present and trustworthy. The student goes at his own pace. In this exercise, he's learning to feel the water hold him up. *He determines the handgrip or lack of one.*

There's no person of normal physical and mental means who cannot overcome any fear of anything, or learn anything if the proper environment of safety and the proper steps are provided. And you're the one who determines what is safe for you. Therefore, no matter how much fear of deep (or shallow) water you have, you can overcome it and be free…and learn to swim with total comfort, confidence and ease.

More fun learning

STEP 65: HOW DO WE FORGIVE?

Here are three ways. There may be more.

If an inno is made and not forgiven, we hold it against ourselves or someone else. We call it a grudge. "Grudge" is too heavy a word here, though. Let's use the word wedge. A wedge in this case is a grudge held against ourselves or someone else. It shows up as a wedge between our body and ourself, or between our body and someone else.

Body, wedge, and myself or the other person

1. Feel where the wedge is being held in your body. It shows up as tension. Where do you find it when you think about what made you afraid in water? Feel the tension now. Give yourself some time to sit with it. Don't be in a hurry if you want healing results.

Sit and feel this wedge, this tension, and let it be there. It may feel like sadness. It may bring tears. This is good: "stuck" (contracted) energy is moving. If you distract yourself and start thinking about something else, that's okay. Just come back and feel it for as long as you're willing.

You may find it helpful to get in touch with the feeling by writing about it: what happened, who was there, how did it make you feel back then, how does it makes you feel now, what did you want to say, what do you want to say now? What has the experience of becoming afraid in water cost you in your life?

By feeling the tension, the wedge, the pain, a teaspoon at a time (I'm not asking you to bite off more than you can chew), and letting it be there without trying to change it, it can begin to move. If you feel it long enough, it will change. It's as simple and certain as 2+2=4. *There's nothing else that can happen.*

You need to feel it, to bring yourself to it, to let yourself be there for it. It may stir emotions. Please allow yourself to feel them to the degree that you're willing. They're okay.

Occasionally in my classes, a student reaches tears. This usually means that something that's been stuck for a long time is moving. Sometimes it means that a belief has broken free: change is happening at its deepest level. It is most welcome.

It may take days or weeks or months to heal this wedge. It's time well spent. Think of how long your wedge has been there, costing you your freedom. "Months" to heal is quick! If you can let yourself sit with the tension of this wedge and feel it for a few minutes every day, taking breaks when you need them, you will, day by day, heal the cause of your fear. This causes a shift in your feeling, a shift in the tension held in your body, an increase in the freedom in your body: it's a physical event. An inner shift causes outer shifts: beliefs→actions→experiences.

2. A second way to heal a wedge is to tell your story about how it came to be, many, many times. Tell it until it no longer holds one iota of charge for you anymore.

Find a person who is willing to listen to your story quietly and without judgment. He or she will not try to talk you out of your feelings. He will not try to "fix" anything. He'll simply listen, with full attention, and be neutral.

If this person gets tired after a number of repetitions, find a second person. Tell the person everything that happened to you. Leave out no detail. As you remember more, include it. Take your time. Talk about who was there, what was said, how you felt, what happened afterward, what you wish had happened, and everything else you remember—even what the weather was at the time.

All that matters is that you feel heard and that you tell the story as many times as necessary until you have discharged the incident 100%. The discharging of this memory is a gradual physical event. The complete discharge of it is a physical event that marks forgiveness. We don't know how long it will take, but we do know that if you stay with it, forgiveness will result.

While you're holding a wedge against yourself or someone else, or while you have pain left over from an incident, your cells carry an electrical charge that came from the incident—from a buildup of all the feelings that were not released or worked through the first time. This electrical charge is emotionally painful.

You can take away the fear, the charge your body has stored by fully feeling the emotions that still remain from the first experience. You can do it also by being gentle with yourself in the water and letting yourself be where you are. Little by little, you work through the old feelings by feeling the "now."

Though you'll still remember that you once had a frightening experience, it will no longer have any power. You'll be free.

A representation of a painful memory stored in your cells:

Cell Wall   Cell Wall   Cell Wall   Cell Wall

The electrical charge of a frightening experience not yet healed is present in every cell of your body.

A frightening experience, healed. You remember that it happened, but the electrical charge is gone. It no longer matters. There is no more pain.

When you tell your story and feel the emotions, letting the stuck energy flow, you discharge the incident. The electrical charge goes away. You will still remember that you had this incident, but it won't matter to you anymore. The charge will be gone.

For forgiveness to take place, follow the steps and give yourself time. Just by beginning the process of overcoming your fear in water, forgiveness steps are being taken. To be reading this book is to have begun the forgiveness process.

> **WE DON'T CARE IF YOU HEAL THE GRUDGE/WEDGE. WE ONLY CARE THAT YOU REMAIN IN YOUR BODY, IN CONTROL.**

As long as you remain in control, you'll be practicing staying in your body. You'll be enhancing your ability to remain in control in other situations. By the way, letting yourself cry is not losing (or giving up) control.

3. The third way you can heal a wedge or heal fear is with affirmative prayer. Since I've seen it work, I would be remiss not to include it. If this idea sends you out of your body, please skip to the next step. We only care that you stay in your body. Stay true to yourself.

Affirmative prayer is a series of heartfelt statements that lead you to knowing that you have done your part to completely forgive the inno that you and/or another person made. It makes use of power you already have. Once you have done your part, the rest is out of your hands. An example of affirmative prayer is this:

"There is only one force, one power, one life in the universe. It is a power of goodness. It encompasses and flows through all things.

I know that this one force, this one life, this one power of goodness lives in me, as it lives in all things. This power in me is mine to use.

I now use this one power to release the inno I made in the water. I forgive myself. I forgive the other person (if there was one) .

I give thanks for the complete freedom I feel from the incident that made me afraid. I give thanks for letting myself off the hook. I give thanks for my confidence, joy, ease, and oneness with myself in the water.

I release this prayer, knowing that it can only produce what I have spoken. And so it is."

You may wish to embellish the statements above to include more detail, though this is not necessary. Keep your added words positive. Expect affirmative prayer to work, like the other ways to forgive above.

STEP 66: HOW TO PREVENT A NEW FEAR FROM SPROUTING UP

You may be wondering, "Can I go back to the pool now?" Yes, you may go back to the pool if you wish, but you're not quite finished. Would you like to know how to prevent a new fear from being born in the future?

HOW TO PREVENT A NEW WEDGE FROM FORMING

Here are two ways to prevent a new wedge from forming. There may be more.

1. When something "bad" happens, you need to experience your feelings about it fully. If you don't, there will be a charge—an electrical charge— left over which, left un-experienced, will likely manifest itself in one of many ways. The sooner you feel the feelings and the emotional (electrical) charge, the less control this experience will have over you later. Correct me if I'm wrong, but I believe *you don't want to carry this with you.*

If you have a new experience of losing control in the water, then when you come out of it, you may soon feel any and all of the following: sadness, confusion, relief, fear, exhaustion, anger, vengefulness, distrust, rage, frustration, pain, gratefulness, hatred, or more. It's best to bring your full presence to each of these feelings—to talk about each of them, to write about each of them, to soak in them and "milk them for all they're worth." Deal with your water episode exhaustively until you have wrung every last bit of energy from it. Take time. I dare say it's some of the most worthwhile time you will have ever spent.

If someone says, "Oh, just get over it," they are not helping you to heal. They are telling you to manage. If just managing fear were satisfactory to you, you would probably not be reading this book. You want more. You owe it to yourself to heal yourself. It's the only predictable way healing can happen. If you wait a few more years, there will likely be more energy built on the incident. You'll have more to heal.

If you had an experience that you remember that made you afraid in water, you came away from it with emotional pain, true? If when you were say, five years old, you had this scary experience and your parents did not allow you to scream and cry, talk about what happened and do what they may have felt was "carrying on" but which was just what you needed to do to fully discharge the energy of the experience, then, unless you have worked it out over the years, you'll have some leftover energy stuck in your body to deal with today. That's the fear you're healing now.

If we all had known this way back when, parents would have been more helpful in those situations and many kids would not have grown up to be adults afraid in water. But since we didn't, at least we have the steps to take now. It's not too late, and the process is just as simple and effective.

2. The second way to prevent a wedge is to interpret experiences in an empowering way. You have a choice about how to interpret a difficult experience. If you interpret it in one way, you'll come away afraid. If you interpret it another way, you'll come away unscathed. This is why many people who have had the same experience you had in the water came away with no fear. In the same way, you've come away from many other experiences unscathed, while others who have had those same experiences came away from them afraid.

After a scary experience, you can either say to yourself, "This happened. It means that I cannot trust myself in this situation. I have proven that I am unsafe here." Or, you can say to yourself, "This happened. There was something I didn't know about handling this situation. Just because I didn't handle it ideally doesn't mean I can't trust myself. It just means I need to learn what I was missing. I need to learn how to stay in my body if this happens again. I forgive myself for my inno. I still trust myself. And now I'll go and get the information I need."

WHAT HAPPENS TO A WEDGE THAT IS NOT REMOVED? (A GRUDGE THAT'S NOT HEALED?)

A wedge that is not healed meets one of several outcomes. A wedge, like everything else, can either expand or contract. If *you* contract, that is, if you tighten further, the wedge expands: it puts more distance between you and your body, or you and someone else.

If it's healed, it transforms into forgiveness. That's an expansion.

If it's kept contracted, it's not healed. It either festers very slowly—in which case you may never see any tangible effects from it—or, it festers more actively. This usually means it turns into a greater fear or a physical symptom, sometimes an injury, sometimes a dysfunction, sometimes an accident or illness or a string of them.

STEP 67: ASK YOURSELF, "DO I WANT TO KEEP THIS WEDGE?"

You may think I'm crazy to ask such a question. But it's a step that cannot be skipped. You may want to continue to hold onto the wedge. This is okay. The important thing is to be in your body about it. Maybe someone is okay about being afraid in water. Really.

If you don't feel good about holding the wedge, then you're slightly out of your body about it. The wedge is keeping you out of your body. A big part of you does not want a wedge. In the long run, it's usually better to be aware of it and take care of it.

How does it serve you to hold it? If you're holding it, it must be serving you. If it weren't, you wouldn't expend this much energy to keep it. To hold it does not mean that you're a bad person, unenlightened, or doing a bad job. It simply means you have probably not examined it as closely as you can.

Do you have any notes to jot to yourself about the wedge? Maybe it's protecting you. Check and see. It protects me by:

_____

_____

_____

What would you rather have in place of this wedge (between your body and yourself)? How would it feel? Can you think of a way to make this feel better? Notes: _____

_____

_____

STEP 68: IT'S NOT YOUR FAULT

If you made an inno, you made it using all the information you had at the time. You did the best you could. You must not fault yourself for that. (Well, you can if you want to.) Would you fault a small child for an error he made innocently, doing the best he could?

You were that small child. Your swimmer-self is that today. Can you see the inno and let yourself off the hook? It was not your fault. What would it take for you to forgive yourself?

To forgive myself, I would have to:

_____

_____

_____

Forgiveness is not just the words, "I forgive you." Those words are worth nothing to you or to your healing unless there's a physical event within you that goes with it.

When we don't forgive, we hold ourselves out of our bodies with the wedge, our unforgiven inno. To forgive means to come back into our bodies.

Body   Wedge/   Self
        Inno

The wedge is the inno we hold against ourselves.
The wedge is fear. Fear keeps us out of our bodies.

Forgiveness is the disappearance of the wedge. Give yourself time.

To Summarize the Healing of Fear

- Fear is born when an inno is made and we don't let ourselves—and perhaps someone else—off the hook for it.

- The reason we don't let ourselves or someone else off the hook for it is that we believe that by not forgiving, we protect ourselves. Additionally, we have no idea how much it will cost us to hold onto it.

- When we study the events of fear, we find that trusting protects us more than fearing.

- When we study the events of fear, we find that there are simple steps to take that gradually and predictably free us from fear.

- When all is said and done, we learn that we truly are innocent.

STEP 69: WHERE WE ARE RELATIVE TO OUR BODIES AT STAGES OF SELF-FORGIVENESS

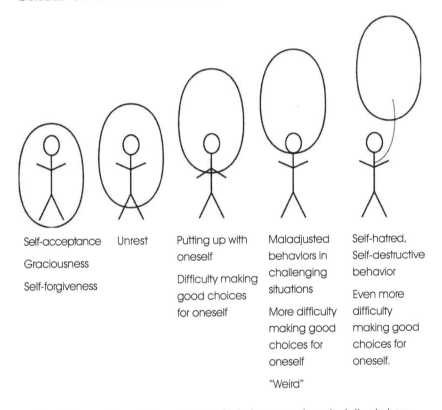

Self-acceptance	Unrest	Putting up with	Maladjusted	Self-hatred,
Graciousness		oneself	behaviors in	Self-destructive
			challenging	behavior
Self-forgiveness		Difficulty making	situations	
		good choices		Even more
		for oneself	More difficulty	difficulty
			making good	making good
			choices for	choices for
			oneself	oneself.
			"Weird"	

The circles and descriptions above refer to how people act relative to how much they have or have not forgiven themselves.

How far down into your body have you come so far toward forgiving yourself for your inno?

Which circle are you in with regard to forgiving your inno? Circle it.

What circle are you in with regard to forgiving any *other person*(s) involved in the incident? Circle it below.

What circle are you in with regard to forgiving
any other person(s) involved in the incident?

How does fear heal? It heals by forgiving yourself and by changing your beliefs. What keeps us from forgiving? Fear. (Yes, it's circular.) Fear that if we forgive, we'll get hurt again. We can't control whether or not we get hurt again—so we may as well just trust and forgive.

Step 70: Preventing Panic, Preventing Drowning

We have discussed what panic is. It's the movement of a person from their first circle out to their fifth circle. Panic is not necessary, once we know what it is and how to prevent it. Preventing it is what this book is about.

What does it mean to drown? Drowning is actually suffocation. It happens when oxygen can't move from the lungs to the blood because water is in the way. It also happens when a person in the water can't get air because his airway is obstructed. Remember, having water in your stomach and having it in your lungs are two different things. In your stomach it's like water you've drunk.

I have no doubt that preventing drowning is virtually equivalent to preventing panic. That goes for adults and for children, age four and over. The drownings of children under four are most often due to parents looking away for "a moment."

If all people knew how to prevent panic, how many fewer drownings would there be? Perhaps ninety percent? Preventing panic comes from knowing how to stay in your body: how to go slowly, how to feel—and obey—your body's signals, and to choose to stay present when you notice that there's an opportunity to leave. This takes practice! (*This* is what swimming and SCUBA classes should spend the bulk of their time on, I believe.) If you're learning the message of this book, you're learning to prevent panic. Now, just practice and become good at it.

USAGE of SWIMMING WORDS

Since you're familiarizing yourself with the culture of swimming, let's examine some swimming words. Often they are misused and misspelled: it may be useful to review them.

A person would not say, "I drowned, and someone rescued me." If someone drowns, we've lost him. Drowning is final. If someone drowned, they would not be telling the story. If someone nearly drowned, they could say, "I nearly drowned," or, "I was struggling for my life..." or, "I felt as though I was drowning."

The exception to this would be a near-death experience where someone actually does drown, is pronounced dead by a physician, and comes back to life. This has happened.

SWIM SWAM SWUM

I swim every day.
Yesterday I swam.
I haven't swum in 30 years.
NOT: I swum yesterday. Or, I haven't swam in 30 years.

SINK SANK SUNK SUNKEN

When I hold onto this brick, I sink.
I sank when I let all my air out.
The boat sank off the coast of Florida.
A boat was sunk off the coast of Florida to create a new SCUBA diving site.
We couldn't see the dock after the storm: it had sunk.
There are many sunken ships off the coast of North Carolina to see while SCUBA diving.

DROWN DROWNING DROWNED

She doesn't want to take a chance that she'll drown, so she's overcoming her fear of deep water.
When he was a child, he witnessed a drowning.
Last year, 4,000 children under the age of four drowned in the United States.
NOT: My cousin drownded when I was five.

BREATH BREATHE

I take a breath before I go under water.
I can't breathe yet when I swim, so I've developed my lung capacity to hold my breath for a lap.

STEP 71: POOL ETIQUETTE

As a swimming student, you may feel as though you are the "low person on the totem pole" at the pool. You aren't! You are doing a noble and worthy thing. Stand tall and proud, and do what you came to do. Others owe you your share of space, as you owe them theirs. Sharing is what is done.

When you choose a time to practice at a pool, you may be able to choose among lap swim periods, free swim periods, adult swimming lessons, or water-walking sessions. If you go to a lap-swim period, you'll want to choose a "slow" lane. The right of way is indeed given to someone swimming laps.

If there's one person in your lane with you, you can share the lane, meaning that each of you takes half the lane: you stay on the left and he swims on the right, for example. If there are already two or more swimmers in the lane, then you'll have to work around them. It's best to avoid lap swimming sessions if there will be more than two of you in the lane. Of course, if the third person arrives and you are sharing the lane with one person, you have a right to stay.

If you're at a water-walking session, ask the person/people in the lane if you can share the space. Your practice space will probably be small at first, but when you begin to swim, you'll need more room.

If you choose a free-swim period when lots of kids are jumping into the pool and there's a lot of noise and activity, you might want to lay claim to a quiet corner. This will show people that this is your space for a while. They may notice and they may not. Your best bet may be to go to a pool during off-hours. Gym pools are typically underutilized much of the time, as well.

STEP 72: CARE AND FEEDING OF YOUR SWIMMING INSTRUCTOR

After you have mastered the information in this book—in other words, you can do everything in it with confidence and ease—you'll be ready to take a traditional beginning swimming class. Perhaps some instructors will consider you more advanced and put you into an intermediate class. At that time, there may be things you know that the instructor is not familiar with. It will be your job to tell the instructor what you need.

It's not that Transpersonal Swimming Institute is the only school that produces students who were once afraid and now can swim freely in the deep. We just don't know of any other schools that teach you how to be in control. *

Here are some guidelines:

1. You might tell your instructor that:

> "X" months/years ago, you were an adult who was afraid in water. You learned that the skill that was missing was the ability to be in control. Now, you have learned how to *be* in control and how to *remain* in control. You're comfortable with the following skills: (list them). You now wish to learn how to do 'Y.' The way you want to learn to do 'Y' is by making your first priority *staying in control* (being comfortable)."

> This way, you'll keep yourself safe in this new environment. It will also bring a new awareness to the instructor, one that we hope all instructors will embrace.

2. As you listen to instructions from an instructor, listen for the things you can do and still remain safe. You may need to translate what he is saying into 2+2=4 language—or an equivalent that feels comfortable to you.

> When he says, "Kick your feet like this," translate that to, "If I can remain in control and be comfortable, kick my feet like this. But control and comfort are more important than what my feet do." *Always* make comfort your first priority, no matter what the instructions are. It's okay to say, "If you don't mind, I'd like to practice comfort first." Hopefully one day, any instructor you choose will tell *you* to be comfortable first.

---

* At the time of this printing, two schools, Orca Swim School in Seattle, Washington and WaterSpirit Swim School in Sausalito, California have been trained and are licensed to teach Miracle Swimming®.

There is one more essential component of learning besides the two that have already been discussed (being in control and having fun/being comfortable) and that is taking responsibility for your own learning. As in any class learning situation, if you take a class, learning depends on the relevance of the material presented, attending all of it, listening, understanding, asking all your questions, applying the teaching, practicing, asking for help when you need it, and giving yourself all the time you need. If you give yourself all these things, you can expect to learn the maximum possible from what is offered.

STEP 73: DISPELLING THE BELIEFS YOU NO LONGER WANT

We've covered your beliefs and the necessity of having beliefs that underlie the experiences you're seeking. This means that some of the beliefs you had at the beginning of this book needed to be replaced.

Some of them may have changed since then. If you'd like to help other beliefs change, you may find it useful to dispel them one by one. If you'd like some help with dispelling them, here are some suggestions. Test your belief until you prove to yourself beyond the shadow of a doubt that it's not true. You'll be able to dispel the following beliefs after you have learned to be in control while testing them.

_____ If I put my face in water, I'll get water in my nose or mouth.

By now you have may have put your face in the water numerous times. You may have learned to keep water out of your nose and mouth or use a nose clip. If you feel that you've achieved control with this skill, the belief has probably already changed. If not, see what happens if, when you remain in control, you put your face in water.

_____ It's dangerous when I get water in my nose or mouth.

This, too, has probably come up more than once. Do you know how to remain in control for this now?

_____ If water gets into my mouth I'll swallow it.

_____ If I get water in my nose or mouth, I'll struggle, sputter, cough, and possibly drown.

You can try letting water into your mouth and seeing if you can remain in control. You don't lose control when you take a drink of water, so perhaps you don't need to lose control at the pool. "But it's a public pool!" you say. Yes, and the health department requires that pool owners maintain a "ten second kill" with its sanitizing chemistry. (It won't hurt your tongue cells.) Everyone gets water in his mouth every once in a while. If the pool is a reputable one and if it's unsafe for any reason and the staff knows about it, you will be called out of the water.

As for letting water into your nose, let's just wait until it happens by accident and see if you can remain in control. It's no fun to let water into your nose on purpose.

_____ I am not a floater.

What is a floater? A floater is someone who is supported by the water when he lies on it, whether his feet are at the surface or at the bottom in shallow water. Again, a sinker is a person who, when he fills his lungs maximally and then lies down on the water, goes to the bottom and doesn't float back up. To see if you're a floater, take that "test," if you can be in control for it.

_____ It would be unwise of me to relax in water.

Why would it be unwise? Test this belief by seeing what happens if you relax completely. You may need to use a nose clip or hold your nose. Don't ask yourself to relax unless you feel it will be safe to do so.

_____ If I relax in water, I'll drop to the bottom like a stone.

Are you willing to relax in water and test this? Go to a comfortable depth to try it. If you think it would be different in deep water, you can test that later when you're ready. Start in shallow water. Remember, we don't care if you test it. We only care that you remain in control. If this isn't possible yet, then I trust you won't perform this test.

_____ I am not a swimmer yet.

Do you think that just because you don't swim, or because you panic in deep water or you get water in your nose, or you can't open your eyes under water, or you sink, or you can't get a breath, or you never passed a swimming test, you weren't born a swimmer? *Impossible.*

When will you think of yourself as a swimmer? When you can dive into the pool and swim a length with easy breathing? When you can tread water, or swim from one place to another without panicking? When you can do X, Y, or Z? That would mean that you believe in the sequence, "Have, Do, Be" instead of Be, Do Have, discussed earlier.

Please consider this idea. Every human being is born a swimmer. You were born with the blueprint to learn to swim, just as you were born with a blueprint to learn to read, drive, walk, talk, etc.

You were shown the steps for reading one by one. You started at the beginning, were given the steps, and mastered the skills so you could read with ease. With swimming, you may well have been given steps out of order—and many of the most important steps were skipped. There was virtually no way to succeed within that system.

There *is* a swimmer within you. The light is on; the shade is simply pulled down. We are raising the shade so your swimmer-self can shine through, which it will surely do if you start at the beginning and skip no steps.

Given these ideas, can you accept, at least intellectually, that you were born a swimmer? If you can, you'll have made a small shift inside you. This shift at the level of your thoughts must ripple out to affect your experience.

_____ I have to push myself in order to learn to swim.

Have you tried anything besides pushing? What would happen if you didn't push—if you allowed yourself to be just where you are? You owe it to yourself to find out. When you do, it may be the first time you've been in the first circle in the water.

_____ If I relax in water, I might lose control.

Can you go to very shallow water where you feel safe and see what happens if you relax? It's okay to leave your hands on the bottom.

If you can't relax, can you feel the tension in your body and let it be there? Just allow it. If it becomes uncomfortable, stand up, or sit up, or take a break. Then do it some more.

_____ I may not have adequate lung capacity to swim.

You may need to test this one later—but if you have already swum (moved from here to there with ease), you can justifiably say that you have adequate lung capacity to swim. You may need to learn how to breathe as you swim.

_____ If I want to learn to swim, I have to follow instructors' directions even if I don't want to.

Hopefully this book is convincing you that you are your own boss when it comes to learning. Only you know what you need in order to feel safe.

_____ Each breath I take must be maximal in case I don't get another one.

In normal situations while you're practicing being in control and learning to swim, and when you become free in water, there should not be any occasion when you would not be able to get another breath. This would only come up in an emergency. In a true emergency, I dare say you'll know if you need to take a maximal breath. But you are in control of preventing the vast majority of emergencies.

Once you know how to stop and stand up, you can get a breath whenever you want in shallow water. Once you know how to roll over on your back and float, staying in your body 100% of the time, you can get a breath whenever you want in deep water. Is it time yet to try one of these? It's only time to do this *if you can stay in your body for it.*

Perhaps you think you could do it, but you wish you had a spotter to help you try it in the deep end. If so, you have reached a milestone: wanting to try it in the deep, believing you can stay in your body with help. Take a moment to acknowledge yourself for this.

If no spotter is available, you can still make progress on your own. Continue to practice rolling over on your back in shallow water. Rest on your back, making sure you are in shallow water where your body is. When you've done this enough, say 100 times (but only you know for sure), you'll be so convinced that you can remain in control any time you do it that you truly will be safe in the deep. Your body will notify you. Then you can practice the roll-over in the shallow and visualize yourself being in the deep. I don't mean to leave your body in the shallow and go to the deep with your thoughts. I mean pretend, by closing your eyes, that you're doing your roll with 8 feet of water below you. Go slowly and stay in your body for it. When you're in control for this, you could ask a lifeguard to watch you practice it in the deep.

_____ To float correctly, my body should be horizontal.

Dispelling this belief requires an understanding of what "floating correctly" means to you. "Correctly" means the position you float in when you're doing literally no work besides holding your breath. Are you doing any work when you float? Decide if your float is correct for you. If you resist a diagonal float for example, it will be stressful. If you let your body float in its natural position, you'll have a float that works and is restful. Use a nose clip, if need be, to remove any concern about water in your nose.

_____ In order to rest, I need the bottom or the side.

If you know how to roll over on your back, you can rest on your back. If you don't, go back to that section. Test whether you need the bottom or the side to rest. See how long you can stay off the bottom and away from the side, for fun. It may be just a few seconds. Notice the time. Even a few seconds may be notable progress.

_____ The water is more powerful than I am.

At what point is it more powerful than you are? Is it more powerful than you when you don't feel in control of yourself? Is it more powerful at any other time? If you're thinking about the ocean, there are times when it's more powerful than we are, but we usually don't go swimming at those times. If you get a surprise from the ocean, the safest you can be is to know how to stay in your body.

Are there any situations in which the water was once more powerful than you, but is no longer? What has changed?

_____ I need to be more physically fit than I am to learn to swim.

To dispel this belief, you just need to learn to swim. You're on your way. If you are a generally healthy person, you do not need to be any more physically fit than you are to learn to swim. The process of learning to swim can be the activity that increases your fitness level. You may visualize huffing and puffing to get to the other side, but this characterizes a swimmer who doesn't yet know how to go slowly and stay in his body. He doesn't yet know that the goal isn't to get to the other side but to remain in control. There's no reason to get winded unless you want to, or unless you aren't paying attention to your comfort.

_____ Other shallow water beliefs that are operating (list them here):

_____

_____

_____

_____ The Miracle Swimming method may work for others but it may not work for me.

To dispel this belief, you'll have to give this book and its contents a try. It has worked for everyone who has tried it since 1983.

You can test any belief you have. I encourage you to test each one, if you can do so safely. If something it too scary to test, break it down into smaller parts.

DISPELLING YOUR UNWANTED **DEEP WATER** BELIEFS

As you dispel your shallow water beliefs, a sweet thing happens. Your mind opens to the possibility that the same things may be true in deep water. You become curious to try them. You're right; the same things *are* true in deep water. Now you need to be able to stay in your body in deep water to experience them.

Being able to stay in your body comes from:

- Practicing staying in your body

- Practicing staying in your body during skills that you used to leave your body for, by doing them only to the point that you can stay in your body—giving yourself full permission to go only this far, and to practice only this much

- Trusting and remaining in trust

_____ I don't trust myself in deep water.

This may be true. You're building a groundwork (infrastructure) of trust in yourself that will expand to deep water if you start at the beginning and skip no steps.

Dispelling your deep water beliefs is a work in progress and you are progressing.

_____ Other deep water beliefs you want to dispel:

_____

_____

_____

_____

How can you test those beliefs?

_____

_____

_____

_____

STEP 74: COMMON MISUNDERSTANDINGS

There are a few common-knowledge phrases that just about everyone has heard about swimming that never should have been taken literally: they are not true. Let's get these straightened out now.

- "Your hands should be cupped when you swim."
- "Your legs should be straight when you kick (knees straight)."
- "You should be horizontal to float correctly."
- "If you're tense, you'll sink."

CUPPED HANDS

As explained earlier, the most efficient position of your hands when you swim or when you pull yourself through the water is open and flat. The flatter the palm of your hand is, the larger the surface area is, and the more purchase you can get on the water: the more water you can push against.

Her cupped hands hinder her somersault.

STRAIGHT LEGS

Instructors who are heard to say, "Keep your legs straight when you kick," don't mean to keep them literally straight. They mean, "straight as compared to bending your knees at 90 degrees or more." If you were to keep your knees straight, you would get zero propulsion from your kick. You could even go backward.

The kick is outside the scope of this book. However, let's put the misunderstanding to rest. The maximum amount of bend in the knees recommended for the flutter kick is shown in the following photo:

This kick will move you. Each leg is in a different phase of the flutter kick.

FLOATING HORIZONTALLY

We have already established that it's not true that the only correct float a horizontal one.

IF YOU'RE TENSE, YOU'LL SINK

You won't sink unless you have no buoyancy. Your body's ability to float depends on your body composition. Your body composition doesn't change suddenly if you become tense. If your neck becomes tense in a back float and it pulls your face below the surface, you'll just pull your face below the surface: you won't sink. I believe that this is what people mean when they say you'll sink.

> Student Marsha said, "When instructors told me that if I was tense, I'd sink, I became afraid to be afraid."

Try this if it sounds like fun. Go into a front float. Then tense up as much as you can. Notice that you don't even approach the bottom. You remain floating but in a tense position.

STEP 75: REVERSALS

Another skill that gives you more freedom in water is the reversal. In a reversal you go from a back float into a front float by almost standing up, but going forward into a front float instead.

Lie on your back in a back float.

Remain still for a while, so that you're totally present in the back float, going nowhere.

Comfortable back float. Notice how relaxed her fingers and feet are.

Then, begin to unfloat by picking up your head and drawing up your knees.

When you pick up your head, take a breath, since soon your face will be going into the water.

After taking a breath, she pulls her
knees toward her head, causing her to rotate.

Finish bringing your face and knees together so that your body is in a ball. You don't have to do anything with your arms or legs.

Your body will have already begun to rotate forward. Instead of standing up, let yourself rotate all the way into your front float. Simply expand from your ball into the front float. Stand up when you need to rest.

With no further movement of her limbs, she allows herself
to continue rolling forward into a front float. She didn't put
her hands out front: that's where they float.

You have reversed your direction and gone from back to front. This is handy if you want to float away from the wall on your back and then return.

Step 76: Comparing Yourself to Others—Reminder

If you find yourself saying, "She can do this better than I can," or "I'm not as good as he is," or "Everyone is learning faster than I am," or "I don't belong here," stop yourself for a moment and examine what you're doing. If there's no charge on your comments, fine (in other words, if your comments are made neutrally with no negativity attached).

Do you *want* to compare yourself to others? Will it help you reach your goals? Does it feel good?

When we compare ourselves to others, we are usually out of our bodies. We are over at theirs (or somewhere else) looking back at ours. That alone is enough to signal that we are making a mistake. If we're not in our bodies, we have lost our presence to what we were doing.

Obviously it's perfectly okay to be out of your body if you're asleep, daydreaming, looking objectively at yourself, or fantasizing something pleasant. It's an inno, however, if you're preventing yourself from being where you want to be.

When you learned to walk and talk, you went at the perfect pace for you. It was the pace that allowed you to find all the nuances of walking and talking, balance, posture, how to shape your mouth, how to form the words, etc., so that you could find your way successfully. In the end, you were perfectly good at walking and talking. If any step had been skipped, it would have taken longer to learn. Or you wouldn't have learned at all. But you learned beautifully.

Can you allow yourself to find your own way with swimming? See if the message of this book fits you. If you follow it, you won't skip any steps— you can only succeed. If you aren't following the steps or you're skipping steps, then you can expect to have some difficulty and perhaps you won't learn. It simply doesn't get any more basic than staying in your body.

If someone else is doing something that you can't do yet, does it mean anything? It may mean that they already learned something you haven't learned yet. Then it's not time for you to do it. You're not "behind." You're where you need to be in order to embody the step you're on. You'll naturally and effortlessly come to the next step.

"Behind and ahead" are terms you can only use when comparing with something or someone else. But your learning is solely based on what is going on within you. So there's no true behind or ahead.

If you say, "But I'm behind where I should be," you're saying there's a standard of performance that you're not living up to in your own mind. You as a spirit are ahead of, or behind your body. In other words, you're out of your body, not in control, and not in the first circle.

I'm behind.

Who says you should be somewhere else? Isn't this standard getting in your way? Does it make you feel good? We aren't in control of when we get there, anyway. If we're not in control—and we aren't in control of when something heals—then wouldn't it be more useful to let yourself off the hook? To stop pushing?

To push on something, you have to be beside it. To push yourself, you have to be beside yourself: next to your body. That means you're *not in* your body.

You must be beside yourself to push yourself.
This is not where you want to be.

Instantly you know that to push yourself is incorrect: it takes you out of your body.

Can you trust that by simply staying in your body you'll reach your goals in the shortest possible time? I hope so. It's true. Letting yourself be where you are is the shortcut to your goals.

STEP 77: WHEN TO PROCEED WITH A NEW STEP VS. PRACTICING MORE

Rule of thumb: if you're not sure whether or not you're ready to go on to the next step, you're not. When you've mastered something, you'll know. There will be no question in your mind. Then the next step will approach *you*.

You may not need to be given the next step. If you've mastered something, and you continue to practice it completely in the first circle, a new thought or whim will cross your mind, a creative idea which will usher you to a new experience. This is how you learned to walk, believe it or not. This is how you, a natural learner, keep learning without being taught. And this is why it's never necessary to push yourself in order to learn.

WHAT LEARNING LOOKS LIKE: THE FIFTH CIRCLE TO THE FIRST CIRCLE

As you know, the steps of going from calm to panic involve going from being in your body to leaving it altogether. It's a process of becoming less and less present until we have virtually no presence at all.

The steps of losing control. © M.Dash 1983

The steps of learning are the exact opposite. They go from having no presence at all (no control) for the skill to being completely present doing it.

The steps of gaining control. The Spiritual Steps of Learning. © M.Dash 1983

When you learn, it seems that you bring new information into your mind and body. Before you learn, there's no *sense* of having this information. After learning, you *feel* different. Something is added. It's added to your mind and it's added to your body.

The "something" that's added is your presence.

What actually happens, I believe, is this. Information is everywhere. There's no spot where *all* information is not. The answer to every question that can be asked is right here and everywhere. It may not be known, but it's here.

Information about how to do x, y, or z is already in your body, but you aren't present to it: you haven't *sensed* it yet. Learning is bringing your awareness to your body to connect with the information that's already there. We say, "I made the connection." When this connection is made, a circuit is closed, exactly like when an electrical circuit is closed and instantly a light bulb to goes on.

As you gradually bring together all the fronts we have talked about in this book, you get closer and closer to closing the circuit. When you bring them together completely, the circuit closes. Instantly you have the breathing. Instantly you have freedom in the deep. You "get it."

When you're out of your body, you can't learn: you can't connect with the information that's there. When you're in your body, the information is "right there." We say, "It just came to me." It's your awareness that came.

Though this happens at a different pace for everyone, the steps are universal. And they can only happen when we're in our bodies, connected to ourselves.

Before learning, you have no *sense* of certain information. There's no connection to it.

No sense of connection to the information

In the second stage of learning, you start to have a mental understanding of something but you can't do it yet:

Beginnings of a mental understanding, a mental connection

In the third stage when you're starting to get it, you're further into your body:

Starting to get it

In the fourth stage when you've almost gotten it, but you know it's "not quite there yet," it looks like this:

Almost have it

In the fifth stage when you've filled your body with awareness down to your toes, you've "gotten it down"—embodied the skill or belief. You've learned it.

Got it

Given this model of learning, how far down into your body have you embodied the belief, "I'm safe in shallow water"? Draw a circle to show how far.

Draw a circle to show how far down into your body you have
embodied the belief, "I'm safe in shallow water."

How far down into your body have you embodied the belief, "I'm safe in deep water"? Draw a circle to show how far.

Draw a circle to show how far down into your body you have
embodied the belief, "I'm safe in deep water."

Does this way of thinking about learning make sense to you?

MASTERY

Remember when the first computers were made? They took up the space of an entire room. A computer that size was needed to do what a laptop computer or a chip can do today.

Our minds work much the same way. When we first learn something, it requires all of our attention. There's no way you could be talking on the phone while you were learning how to walk on a tight rope. There's no way we can learn two things at once although it's attempted by many people daily. It just doesn't work. Go ahead and try to think of an example of learning two things at once. I suggest that either both went unlearned, or only one was actually learned. When you add the factor of fear for your life, you can easily see that "you must be present to learn."

238

When we allow ourselves to give our full attention to what we're learning, we learn beautifully. We ask our questions. They're answered. We go to the next level of understanding. We take the next risk because it's fun. We grow. Our presence becomes reliable. The skill becomes reliable.

Once we've learned something, the amount of attention required to do it is much less than when we were first learning it. Let's say that once we learn it, we can do it with one quarter as much attention, which is the same as saying one quarter as much *presence*. It requires little presence to do a skill when we've learned it.

When we've mastered it, it's something we can do with almost no presence whatsoever. We can do it "on automatic." This is why people can use lap swimming as a form of meditation. They are far from (notice the location: far) having to think about their safety, their buoyancy, their stroke, or their breathing. They have mastered these things so that they can now "go" different places with their thoughts.

The picture that we would add to the series of circles above is this:

Mastery

The skill takes up very little attention: very little space in your presence.
Notice the small circle at the chest.

The small space that mastery takes up is not really located in your chest or in any one section of your body as this diagram suggests. This is simply a representation of the tiny space mastery takes up, relative to the larger circles in the previous diagrams.

Just as your presence as a spirit is in every cell of your body, mastery is located in every cell of your body. But the presence of mastery is tiny in each cell compared to the majority of space in each cell that your presence requires when you're in the midst of learning something. This change in your cells, called mastery, builds infrastructure.

THE NECESSITY OF STAYING IN YOUR BODY

How are you doing with the teaching in this book? Do you believe that it's more important to stay in your body at all costs than it is to learn a swimming skill? Do you understand?

Let's review.

- In order to learn, you must feel safe.

- If you feel safe, you feel in control in the moment. You have your survival needs taken care of and you have attention to spare for something else.

- If you feel safe, you have attention for learning.

- The reason you haven't learned what you wanted to learn in the past is that you didn't feel safe and you didn't feel in control.

- The "anatomy" of feeling safe and being in control is that you're in your body: you and your body are in the same space.

- The process of losing safety and losing control is the movement of you from your body outward (out of your body).

- The way to prevent "losing it," that is, losing control or losing your presence of mind, is to keep yourself in your body on purpose.

- The way to stay in your body on purpose is to deliberately go slowly and *feel*.

- There are two optimum speeds: Slow and Stop. If you feel uncomfortable, stop. Stop until you feel comfortable again. Then go slowly. You can be in a race and still be slow on the inside.

- What you *feel* guides you as to what to do now. Your feeling tells you when to stop. You don't need to know what to do later. You only need to know what to do now.

- If you feel yourself speeding up inside, your feeling is telling you there's a belief that you're in danger. It's telling you to slow down or stop so you can remain in control and check it out.

- Every time you've learned something, you've been in your body. (Check to see if you can find any exceptions.)

- To guarantee your success in learning *anything*, you simply need to keep yourself in your body.

If you have reached this part of the book and you haven't yet mastered the topics and skills that have been covered, go back. Take your time. Don't push yourself. As you can see, pushing doesn't work with overcoming fear. Don't you owe it to yourself to give yourself a chance? To allow yourself to be completely present for each part?

STEP 78: JUMPING IN

Would you like to be able to run off the deck and jump into the deep end doing a cannonball, like a kid? No? Fair enough. How about gently slipping into the pool off the edge? If you start at the beginning and skip no steps, it's inevitable that you'll be able to do either of these in a while. Let's start at the beginning.

In shallow water, chest deep or less, hop up and down.

- As you hop, notice what parts of your body are being used most: the balls of your feet, your thighs, knees, ankles and hips. As your weight comes down onto your feet and the bottom of the pool, your joints absorb most of the force. They make your landing soft on your feet and on the rest of your body.

- As you hop, turn around a full 360 degrees. Notice that you don't need to be taught how to do this.

- Now hop, turning the other way.

- Now hop a little higher. When you hop higher, you'll land with a little more weight on your feet. This requires that you bend your knees a little more to absorb your weight. It also requires that your other joints absorb a little more, too. Notice these changes. This is how you protect your body when you jump. When you jump into a pool, your joints will absorb a little *more* of your weight so that you land safely.

- Always land on your feet. Only when you jump into deep water (9-10 feet) would you *not land* on your feet—you probably wouldn't land on the bottom at all.

- When you've become accustomed to jumping higher, visualize yourself jumping up *so* high that you'd go under water when you landed in order to land softly. See yourself doing this a number of times.

- When you can see this in your mind and you're ready, try it. It doesn't matter whether you jump that high or not: just practice landing as though you had. When you go under water, it's a good idea for now to use a nose clip or hold your nose.

- When you've done this many times, ask yourself if you're ready to try this from a sitting position on the side of the pool. If not, fine.

- If yes, sit on the deck near the edge. Put one hand on the edge and one on your nose. Give yourself a "scoot" off the deck and land on your feet gently, absorbing your weight with your joints. It's okay to leave one hand on the deck as you enter.

How did it go? Practice it 20 or 30 times over your next few pool visits.

STEP 79: GETTING OUT OF THE POOL

There's the obvious way out of the pool: use the ladder or steps. Then there's jumping out which is sometimes more convenient. This takes a few practices to make it smooth (making it one of the quickest things to learn) but it may take doing it a 15-20 times in a week to gain the strength for it. The strength comes surprisingly soon if you stick with it for a few days.

Place your hands on the deck, or, if the deck is too high, on the gutter.

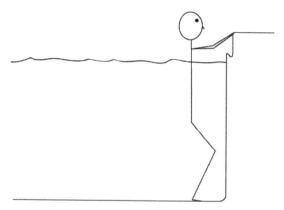

Place your hands on the deck, or, if the deck is too high, on the gutter.

Jump up, press down on the deck/gutter with your hands, and straighten your elbows. Up you go.

243

Put your knee on the deck or gutter and climb up to the deck.

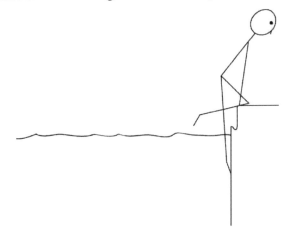

Climbing out of the pool without the ladder

If you need to put your hands in the gutter rather than on the deck, your knee will go onto the gutter, too. It may take you an extra step to climb out, but it will work.

MILESTONE

At this point, you've covered all the basic skills in shallow water that enable you to play and explore in shallow water safely. The most important of these skills is staying in your body. You've covered them all: now take time to master them. Give yourself a standing ovation!

When you have done this, you can take yourself and your new infrastructure to the deep end. If you wish to visit the deep end before you've mastered the shallow end skills, please do what's fun.

STEP 80: DEEP WATER

As one student says in our video,

> *"Deep water is more fun now. Shallow water is boring."*
> —Ram

It's possible to learn to be comfortable in deep water without ever going into it. It's a perfectly good way to become 100% calm about deep water. You won't be able to show anyone that you've gotten deep water under control without a deep end, but you can know beyond the shadow of a doubt for yourself. Do you believe this? _____

To do that, practice the front and back floats in the shallow water until you've become so anchored in your body and you've tested the water's buoyant force so many times and in so many conditions that you've convinced yourself that it's reliable and it's never going to change. This would be some (more) of the most worthwhile time you ever spent in your life, I dare say. Though I have only given one paragraph to that suggestion, I could end the book here. It truly is a worthy pursuit.

If you have a deep end at your pool, then if and when your curiosity gets the best of you and there's someone else at the pool with you, head for the deep. Holding onto the gutter/wall, make your way slowly, hand over hand, toward the deep water. As you go, check in with yourself. Am I in my body? Am I in the second circle? Is this fun? Stop and regroup if you get ahead of yourself. Stop and stay at the depth where you can be comfortable while still holding on.

Ahead of yourself   Comfortable

> WE DON'T' CARE IF YOU GO INTO THE DEEP END.
> WE ONLY CARE THAT YOU FEEL IN CONTROL
> AND ARE HAVING FUN.

No pushing. If you're in control and having fun, it's only a matter of *when* you want to go to the deep end, not "if." The time will come. But if you're never ready, that's okay, too.

Remember what Sylvia said:

> *"If I know I can't put my feet on the bottom, I panic. I can fake it for a while, but then the truth comes and gets me."*

She knew it wasn't time to go to the deep end yet: she couldn't remain in control.

When you have gone as far as it's fun to go toward the deep end, stop and feel your feelings. Are you totally calm? Great! Would you like to rest here for awhile? Put your face in? Just have fun.

Or, is your heart beating faster than normal? Is there any tension in your body? These are both okay, as long as you're still having one of the two kinds of fun.

Let your heart beat as quickly as it wants to beat. Let your tension be there. Is it in your hands? Your arms? Your gut? Just feel it and allow it. Stay there as long as you are curious about it. If it's not okay, go back toward the shallow end or all the way to the shallow: it's not time to be in the deep. Go back and practice things that are comfortable in the shallow end, or if you're satisfied, call it a (successful) day.

2+2=4
IT'S OKAY NOT TO BE READY TO LEARN IN THE DEEP END

WHY RETURN TO THE SHALLOW END TO PRACTICE SOMETHING I'M ALREADY COMFORTABLE DOING?

Remember: it's useful to practice something you're already comfortable doing because you can still bring more of your presence to it (unless you've mastered it). This was discussed in the section entitled "What Learning Looks Like..." (Step 77). Therefore, if you go back to the shallow end, you can still make progress. The fun you have will either teach you, or heal you.

If you decide to remain in the deep end, what, if anything, feels different about being in the deep? Often people say, "I can't feel the bottom," or, "I feel more buoyant." What do *you* feel?

Make an agreement with yourself now. Promise, *I will not let go of the wall today.* That's just for now. Agreed? We want you to feel safe and to know you can stay in control.

STEP 81: FEELING THE DEEP WATER HOLD YOU UP ON YOUR FRONT

If it sounds like fun, keeping your grasp of the wall in the deep end, lower your face into the water and let your body dangle. Let the water hold you in a front float. Your hands will prevent you from drifting away. But they shouldn't support you: the water will. You won't kick your feet up behind you (right?) because you know that letting your feet go where they naturally go is the best way to find your natural float.

How does it feel? Does it feel the same as your float in shallow water, or different?

Spend some time in this float, coming up to rest whenever you want. Is there's any tension as you float? Let it be there. What happens?

Right, it disappears. If it hasn't disappeared, then guess what? You must be in a hurry, or you're pushing yourself. Remember, it's okay to go back to shallow water if being in the deep does not allow you to slow down inside.

Give yourself many minutes over several days to feel the deep water holding you up. It takes a while for most people to believe it. You want to believe it in your gut. You want to embody the belief that you float in deep water. Prove it to yourself, without letting go of the wall.

You probably want to know if the float will work if you let go, as well. There will be a time soon when you can experiment with that. And when the time comes, what do you think you'll find out? One way to test it is to put your clasped hands behind the ladder's side-rail, and feel yourself float.

The certainty that deep water holds you up (just as shallow water does) is a knowing that you have probably sought for a long time. *Give yourself time to absorb this knowing.*

IF YOU FEEL MORE BUOYANT IN DEEP WATER THAN IN SHALLOW

Often people report feeling more buoyant in the deep water than in the shallow. How can this be? The water's density is not different between the shallow and deep. Your body's density isn't different between shallow and deep. So the relationship between the two densities isn't different between the shallow and deep, either. Therefore, physics says your buoyancy is exactly the same in both shallow and deep. Yet people commonly *feel* more buoyant in the deep.

If you're in the shallow end, you're always aware of the bottom. You always know it's there in case you want it. If you're always aware of it, some of your presence is always there. Some of *you* is at the bottom. The rest of you is at the top. You're split. The two parts of you pull to be together, like magnets.

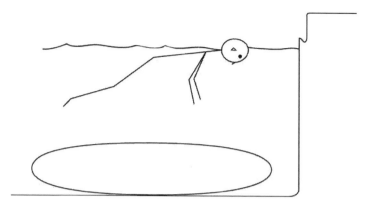

You and your body are in two places. There's a pull to unify.
You feel a pull toward the bottom.

If you feel pulled by the bottom, it's because so much of your attention is on the bottom.

If you feel more buoyant in the deep end, it's because you're not wishing for, or depending on the bottom to help you stand up or rest. You've let go of using it. You've let go of your attachment to it. This letting go allows you to be fully at the surface with your body. You and your body are at the top. You feel lighter, more buoyant than in the shallow end.

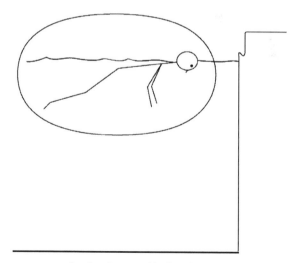

Feeling buoyant in the deep
Eventually, you'll also disconnect from the bottom in the shallow.

Since the use of the bottom to get air is not possible in the deep, learn to remain at the surface with your body. Eventually, you'll also disconnect from the bottom in the shallow.

STEP 82: ELEVATOR GAME

How far down into your body have you embodied the belief, "Deep water holds me up?" Go to the deep end ladder. *If it sounds like fun, keeping yourself vertical,* take a breath and climb down the ladder as far as you would like to go. If your feet start to float up behind you, it's okay: you forgot to stay vertical. The game will still work. If you want to stay vertical, you'll have to adjust your alignment and posture to keep your feet directly under you as you descend. Go slowly and feel what you have to do to stay vertical. See how far you can have fun descending.

We don't care if you go down the ladder even one rung. We only care that you remain in control and have fun.

When you have descended as far as you're comfortable, you may notice that there's pressure on your ears. This is normal. The deeper you go, the more pressure there is on any airspace in your body. Your ears are the place you feel it most. If the pressure bothers you, come back up the ladder a rung or two to relieve it. If you have a cold, or are getting one, you may feel it at only 2 to 3 feet of depth.

When you're as deep as you want to go on the ladder, try this test. Remember: we don't care if you do this—only that you feel completely in control and are having fun.

Loosen your grip on the ladder, but not enough to let go of it completely (unless you'd like to). Expect this: the water will push you back to the surface as though you're on an elevator. It's a free ride. They say there's no "free ride." But they didn't know about deep water. It's always a free ride up when you're under water and you have air (unless you're a sinker).

Be like a kid. Take this ride a hundred times. "Watch me, Mom!" Spend lots of time doing this. Prove to yourself that the water pushes you up when you have air. Isn't this something you want to know? Give yourself time to prove it beyond the shadow of a doubt. It may take a few days. Be considerate of others who may want to exit and enter the pool at the ladder.

STEP 83: VERTICAL FLOAT

At the ladder, if it's not getting too much use by others, experiment with keeping your body floating in a vertical position. You can hold onto the ladder.

Floating vertically is a first step toward bigger things that shall remain unnamed for now. Start by taking a breath and holding it, as always. To float straight up and down you'll have to keep your body aligned, head above spine, spine above hips, and hips above knees. If your head is tilted forward, you'll tip forward into a front float. If it's tilted backward, you'll go into a back float. Line yourself up vertically at the ladder or wall and see if you can balance as though you were standing on the water.

- Align your head directly above your spine.
- Keep your feet from going up behind you (or ahead of you) by keeping your thighs and knees below your spine. It takes some balancing.

Getting ready for a vertical float. He's making sure that
the water is holding him up, not his hands.

251

Below, a vertical float at the wall in the deep:

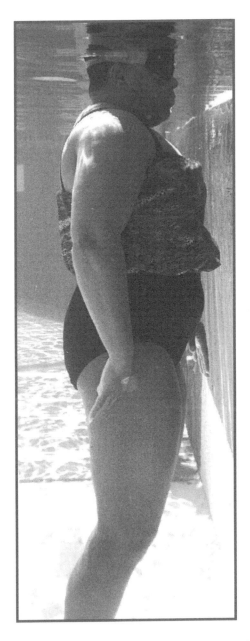

She knows that the water will hold her up, so she's comfortable
with her arms at her sides. She aligns herself vertically.

Away from the wall once he knows he can remain in control, the student below "stands on the water" or "hangs from the surface."

Vertical float, midpool. Aligned from head to foot.

If you find yourself tipping forward or backward, ask yourself if you're letting your head drop forward or backward.

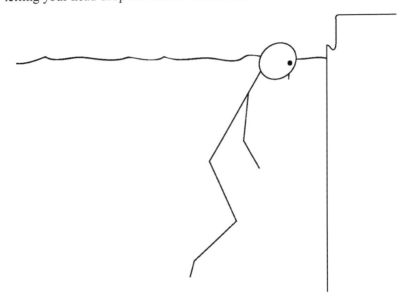

Head tipped forward leads you into a front float.
Of course, your front float may be more horizontal than this.

One of the first things you'll notice as you experiment is that you don't sink. *You remain afloat.* Yes, you. There you are, the top of your head and perhaps even some of your forehead or face, out of the water. The more air you have and the more buoyancy you have, the higher you'll float. Spend some time with this new feeling in deep water. Let it sink in. Part of learning is being pleasantly surprised, marveling at how this could possibly be so after all these years of thinking otherwise, reveling in the wonder of the truth, and watching your expectation of what will happen next time change to what really happens. You're getting the picture! This is an example of moving your foot from one rung on the ladder *toward* the next one. A lot is happening here.

Reminder: if you're in a vertical float and your nose is below the water, don't tip your head back: you'll get water in your nose.

254

If You're a Sinker (Vertical Float)

If you're a sinker, you won't be able to stay at the surface for the previous exercise. To make yourself as buoyant as you can be (which is not buoyant), take the maximum amount of air you can comfortably hold. Remember being a sinker is not a problem. It just means you'll learn to stay afloat by other means. The means are coming soon. Only experiment in deep water if you know you can be in control to come back up.

For a sinker, the exercise above is about taking a good breath and allowing yourself to sink. You can do this in water that's 6 feet deep if you want to be able to stand on the bottom and reach the deck. Or, you can sink all the way to the bottom in the deep end. Someone should be watching you as you experiment with this. They should have a pole to extend to you in case you need assistance there at the bottom. But you and I know (right?) that you wouldn't try something that you can't be in control for.

Or, in deep water, you can stop your sinking by holding onto the ladder at the depth you want to stop. Do what's comfortable for you. You can bring yourself back up the ladder at any time. Monitor your air, so you feel safe. Come up while you still have plenty of air.

Go down the ladder or to the bottom many times. Remember, we only care that you feel 100% in control and safe.

If you can use your arm sweep to swim back to the surface, that's another option. You can also jump off the bottom to go up.

If it sounds like fun, once you're on the bottom and feeling safe, take a moment to look around. Check out the new view. The world looks different from the bottom of the deep end. Few people—in all of humanity—have seen it.

STEP 84: FEELING THE DEEP WATER HOLD YOU UP ON YOUR BACK

In the deep end, review all the exercises that remind you that deep water holds you up. Each time you go to the deep end, it pays to review this feeling and anchor it further into your body.

To feel the water hold you up on your back, hold onto the deep end wall again and let your body be flush with the wall: your chest, stomach, thighs, and toes will all be touching it.

Begin this way:

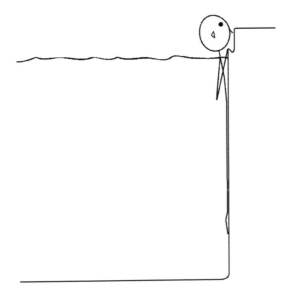

Remember: keep your body flush against the wall.

Lean back a bit and lower yourself down into the water so that your ears are in. Don't let go of the wall. Let yourself be completely supported by the water, not by your hands. The water will hold you up (unless you're a sinker). Your hands simply keep you from drifting away.

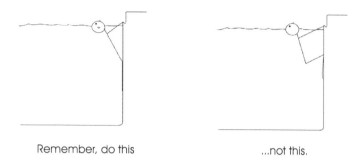

Remember, do this   ...not this.

Now, take a breath and hold it. What happens?
Now let your air out. What happens now?

Take a comfortable breath, and hold it. Practice back floating at the wall and become comfortable with it.

If you'd like to try breathing in a back float, notice that as you breathe, your floating level changes, as it did in the shallow end. If you inhale a lot of air, you rise. If you exhale a lot of air, you drop. If you exhale too much, you could go below the surface if you aren't paying attention. But I know you *are* paying attention so, you prevented yourself from going somewhere you would not be comfortable (under water on your back where you would get a snootfull if you weren't wearing a nose clip).

To float for a while in a back float with your hands on the wall like this, you need to find a level of air-exchange that allows you to stay at a comfortable "altitude." Most people will need to breathe somewhat shallowly. If you breathe too deeply, your altitude will vary too much and you'll submerge.

If you're very buoyant, you can breathe normally and your altitude will remain comfortable. If you aren't very buoyant, you may need to hold all your air in your lungs in order to float. There's something you can do to make up for this.

STEP 85: FOR SINKERS, THERE'S SCULLING

If you're not buoyant and you float vertically but only with a maximal breath, or, if you're a sinker, go to a depth where you feel 100% safe. Then, go into a back "float," such as it is. You'll need to hold as much air as you can possibly hold. Your feet will rest on the bottom, which is natural for you.

If you're fighting the fact that your feet are at the bottom, feel how much energy you're using to fight the natural laws. It's not time to learn sculling yet (which is defined in the next paragraph). It's time to lie in the water diagonally or vertically using a nose clip and allowing your feet to be on the bottom, without any resistance. When you can do this, even though you are going to sink, you'll be in the first circle for the first time with this back "float." Then, you'll have a chance to make progress. You can learn how to stay up.

Sculling is a movement you make with your arms and hands that gives your body lift in the water, whether or not you're buoyant. If you use it during a back float, it will prevent you from sinking, even if you're a sinker. Remember, the Olympians need to stay up somehow when they're not swimming from here to there. This is how they do it.

When you're in a back float...

- if you push downward, where will that take you? _____
- if you push upward, where will that take you? _____
- if you push backward (toward your head), where will that take you? _____
- if you push forward (toward your feet), where will that take you? _____

In the water, you'll find that:

- pushing downward takes you up

- pushing upward takes you down

- pushing backward takes you forward

- pushing forward takes you backward

- pushing downward gives you the lift you want to reach the surface, but the lift is only temporary if you're a sinker. It disappears after the downward push. To stay afloat if you're a sinker, you need a movement that delivers constant lift.

In shallow water, go into your back float, such as it is.

A sinker on his way to sculling. He's almost there: his hands need to be pitched downward more in order to get the lift he needs. See photos below for correct hand angles.

Sweep your hands back and forth from the 3:00 and 9:00 to 6:00 and back to 3:00 and 9:00. Turn your wrists at the end of each sweep so that you're always pushing on the water with your pancake palms. Remember, your palms are your power surface.

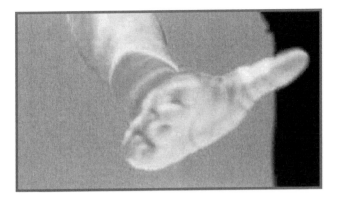

An angle between 0 and 90 degrees: This angle gives you lift when your palms sweep sideways on the water (in this case, if she sweeps to our right).

Back and forth: pitch your hands like this.
The slight cupping in his left hand makes that hand less effective.

Good pitch for hands while sculling. This pitch used while she sweeps back and forth in her back float will keep her up. Her palms could be flatter.

If you keep your palms (hands) pitched at the correct angle for you (between 0 and 90 degrees) you'll be able to keep yourself from sinking. Bingo.

How does it work? To get the lift from your arm sweep and pitched hands, you need to create at least a little downward force all the time. You create this not by pushing your hands toward the bottom of the pool, but by pitching your hands, as above. In each of your arm sweeps, because the effect of your pitched palms causes pressure both sideways *and* downward, and the movement of your palms is constant, you'll get constant downward force and therefore, constant lift. This will keep you in a back float position where you can breathe and rest.

Practice this every day you go to the pool, once you've reached this level of comfort. If you focus on staying in your body, feeling the pressure on your palms, you'll improve your lift every day.

TROUBLESHOOTING SCULLING

What if your hands were vertical, as in the photo below? If they pushed away and pulled back toward you pitched at 90 degrees, they would give you zero lift: there would be no downward force.

What not to do. At 90 degrees the hand pushes only sideways on the water. This gives no lift. Additionally, her thumb position is keeping her palm from being flat.

If you hold your hands horizontally so that they slide through the water sideways without getting any purchase on it at all, this too will give you no lift.

Sliding the edges of your hand through the water gives you no lift.

If you're less buoyant, your hands need to be less pitched (more horizontal than vertical). If you're more buoyant, they can be more pitched (more vertical than horizontal).

STEP 86: THE CONTROL METER

Rate your level of control on the Control Meter. To what degree are you in control in shallow water?

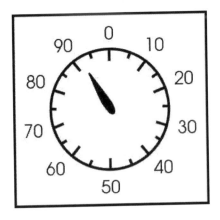

Control Meter

Are you 50% in control in shallow water? 100%?

What percentage of time are you completely in control in shallow water? In deep water?

Each lesson in this book is about being in control. You can imagine a meter that measures your level of control for each thing you do in the water, whether it's walking across the pool, lying on your back holding onto the wall, or letting go in deep water. The divisions of the meter mark increments of control and comfort. One hundred percent control is mastery: the embodiment of control and peacefulness.

Only do that which allows you to be in control all the time in the water.

> WHEN OVERCOMING FEAR, IT'S MORE ADVANCED TO REMAIN IN CONTROL AND ABORT A SKILL THAN TO COMPLETE THE SKILL AND LOSE CONTROL

Your Learning

As we saw at the Learning Meter, the quality of the learning can be very high if our questions are answered and we're given steps that meet us exactly where we are. We are able to be successful and make progress. This is high quality learning. On the other hand, if we are consistently given steps that are too advanced or too elementary for us, or we don't get answers to our questions, we are not being met at our level and learning quality is low.

There are several components of learning. They're listed in the table below. Depending on what happens in each of these components, your learning quality will vary.

Once you're aware of the information in the table, you can make an informed choice about your approach to your learning.

LEARNING QUALITY TABLE

LEARNING QUALITY LEVEL		
Low	**Medium**	**High to Mastery**
FEELING Tension	Ease	Oneness with water
INTERNAL SPEED OR FREQUENCY High speed High frequency	Low speed Low frequency	Stillness
PRESENCE Second to fifth circles	First circle most of the time	Full presence for X: could do Y at the same time
NECESSITY OF RETURNING TO YOUR BODY High Must return often	Low Can return when needed	Very low Can return when needed
PHYSICAL SKILLS Performed fast and with tension	Performed more slowly with little tension	Performed slowly, with ease, efficiency
AMOUNT OF FUN Not fun Pushing, Frustration, self-doubt	Willing. Fun most of the time	Play. Joy, Can be meditative

LEARNING COMPONENT

Progression of learning quality from low to high over six learning components.

STEP 87: PLAY

Why are games and toys not just important, but necessary? During games and toys, you build confidence in yourself in various unpredictable situations. As you learn how to stay in your body, you learn *how to be safe: in control.* You learn about balance. You learn what the water does for you and what you must do for yourself. You develop a new relationship with water. It sparks your curiosity and brings new realizations.

If you've ever tried before to put together the breath, float, arm stroke and kick, it most likely didn't work. It may not have worked because:

- you probably weren't in your body

- you probably weren't in your body for any two of them at once

- you didn't have an understanding of how the water and your body work together

- you didn't believe that the water would hold you up

- you were worried about your safety

Experimenting at your level of confidence is fun. Finding the answers to your questions is fun. By following what's fun, you expand your understanding of the water. By practicing being in your body, your body and you become organized: you can now bring your *whole being* to the table. When you have these two components under your belt—having fun and being in your body—you learn to swim.

GAME: POSITIONS

In shallow water, create and get into five new positions in the water that you could not accomplish on land. Use a nose clip.

> DO WE CARE IF YOU GET INTO FIVE POSITIONS? NO. WE ONLY
> CARE THAT YOU STAY IN YOUR BODY FOR EACH POSITION YOU TRY.

STEP 88: CHECK IN

How are you doing? Do you understand everything so far? Have you done the exercises? Are you finishing the book so you can go back and do the exercises?

If you follow your desire and do what's fun, no matter what it is, you'll learn in the best way. My two hopes are that you won't skip any steps and that if you have a question, you'll ask it: either look back in the book (use the index to find topics easily), or experiment.

If you find yourself feeling far better in the water than you ever have before, you may conclude that you're "there"—and you may be. You've made vast improvements. Check for full comfort, though: sometimes a student who says he feels fine is still tense. He feels fine in comparison to how he felt in the past. But compared to how calm he could feel, he still has a way to go. Just check your feelings and get your body's feedback. If you're calm, you know it.

THE NECESSITY OF REST

When you get enough rest, you function best. When you rest, you can feel "hunches." You can hear new ideas when they bubble to the surface. You have the opportunity to listen to them and follow them.

If you go, go, go all the time without stopping, you deny yourself natural shortcuts that are yours for the taking but which can't get through to you when your mind is too busy. When you stop, you're more receptive. It's necessary to rest often as you learn.

At the pool, do what's fun. Make it easy for yourself.
You'll learn beautifully.

STEP 89: REMEMBER THIS IF YOU'RE FEELING STUCK

Our natural rhythm is to expand and contract, expand and contract. We naturally expand when we're patient with ourselves, trust, go slowly and stay true to ourselves. Feeling "stuck" does not feel like expansion. In fact, it's a contraction. There's nothing wrong with contraction. But sometimes it doesn't feel good. If you feel stuck, knowing what it's about can help you to expand again. A contraction comes when a belief we have, whether we're conscious of it or not, stands in the way of expansion.

If you're feeling stuck, check to see if you're using the laws of learning favorably:

- Are you having fun?
- Are you practicing comfort rather than a skill?
- Are you pushing yourself?
- Are you practicing while frustrated?
- As you practice, are you "speeding" inside?
- Are you practicing while you're feeling any concern, worry or fear?
- Have you asked for a spotter when you wanted one? (If one is not available, it doesn't mean you can't make progress.)
- Do you have a question that hasn't been asked?
- Is there a nagging thought that hasn't been addressed?
- Are you criticizing yourself? Comparing yourself to others?
- Do you agree with the laws of learning that this book teaches?

The resolution of each of these questions brings you back into your body. You can only learn while you're in your body.

- If you're not having fun, what *would be* fun?
- If you're practicing a skill, are you willing to practice comfort instead?
- If you're pushing yourself, are you willing to let yourself be where you are?
- If you're speeding, can you slow down to a stop?
- If you're practicing frustration, would you change the subject or go backward?
- If you have a concern or worry, have you asked a spotter to cover it for you?

- If you have a question, will you ask it of someone who knows the answer?

- If there's a nagging thought, will you voice it?

- Do you feel safe to speak up?

- If you're criticizing yourself or comparing yourself to others, you're outside of yourself looking back from another place. Are you willing to come back to your body? To feel?

In this book you're relearning a way to learn. If it doesn't feel like your way, use what you can and leave the rest. The important thing is your comfort.

STEP 90: BREATHING PRACTICE

Let's review breathing. Go to the shallow end of the pool. Hold onto the wall with one or both hands if it will help you feel 100% comfortable. Being 100% in control is essential. Notice your breath for a minute. Notice the duration of your inhalation and the duration of your exhalation. Notice whether you're breathing through your nose or mouth. Both are okay.

Visualize yourself inhaling through your mouth and exhaling into the water through your nose. The inhalation will begin, obviously, while you're standing up. The exhalation will begin before your face goes into the water. It will continue as long as you have plenty of air to blow out. It will end after you come back above the surface, just before you take a new breath. By the time you take your new breath, you will have felt the exhalation complete itself. You would not want to take a new breath before the old one was out. This would make you winded. Find a comfortable exchange of air. When you can imagine yourself doing this, go ahead and do it. Go slowly.

> DO WE CARE IF YOU EXHALE INTO THE WATER AND INHALE AS
> ABOVE? NO, WE ONLY CARE THAT YOU FEEL IN CONTROL.

Remember, if your breath gets stuck (it stops coming out) or if you swallow, let it happen. Don't try to change it. You're getting into your body little by little and you need to let these things straighten themselves out. They will do so most quickly if you simply allow yourself to observe what's happening and trust it. You will come further and further into your body. Don't criticize. Give yourself time.

This exercise of going under water to exhale and coming up to inhale, repeatedly, is called bobbing.

STEP 91: SWIM STOP SWIM

This exercise is unrelated to the breathing exercise above. For this exercise, you—and your body—should be in the shallow end of the pool.

From your comfortable front float, practice swimming a few strokes as you hold your breath. Stand up when you need air. Do this a number of times, so it feels natural and familiar again.

Then, do it again, but this time, after you've swum a couple of strokes, stop everything. Let your body find its equilibrium position—the position it ends up in when you do nothing. It may take 5 seconds or so for your body to find equilibrium. Are you comfortable with the amount of air you took?

Your body may reach equilibrium in a horizontal position. It may reach equilibrium in a diagonal or vertical position. Just give it time to get there.

After you have rested in equilibrium for a few seconds, resume swimming. Simply reach out front again and use your arm sweep to propel you forward. If you have attention to place on your palms, feel them as you sweep. These are your points of connection with propulsion. Yes, the inside surface of your arms also press on the water, but it's your palms' effect that's most powerful.

You may wonder where this exercise leads. It is about balance and control. Everything in this book contributes to advancing one or more fronts. Advancing the fronts to their endpoints leads to closing the circuit of all the fronts of learning to swim.

STEP 92: APPROACHING THE WALL

Often when students swim, they become uncomfortable as they get close to the wall. They feel themselves start to feel tense and hurried. Have you found this, yourself?

The cause of this is usually that the swimmer reaches the wall before her body arrives. She is ahead of her body. To cure this, as you swim toward the wall, keep yourself back where your body is. This means *feel* as you swim. Go slowly and stay in your body. Enjoy the whole ride. No beating your body to the wall. When you reach the wall, you'll be able to calmly put your hand up to it rather than grabbing it.

STEP 93: SKIPPING TIME

Let's talk more about the experience above of swimming toward the wall and finding yourself scrambling to grab it. Let's talk about any time you practice something and you feel yourself speeding up inside, and have to stop the skill because it's gotten away from you.

When this happens, there's a point when everything happens very quickly. You can't control it. It gets too scary and you "go away." First you go away...then, the skill falls apart. While it's apart, you envision a remedy (safety). That is, you go to safety. When your body reaches safety, it catches up with you, so you and your body are together again: you feel safe.

You move before your body does.

It's working.   It fell apart.

What fell apart? You and your body.

It was the unison of body and spirit that fell apart. It wasn't the skill that got away from you. It was *you* that got away from you.

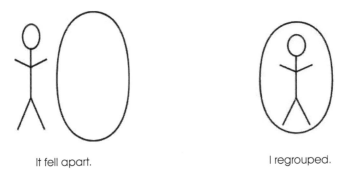

It fell apart.   I regrouped.

When you leave your body like that, there are a few milliseconds of time that you can't account for. You missed them. Though someone on the deck might be able to describe what you did, you can't: you weren't there. You might say, "I don't know. It happened too fast."

You didn't skip time on purpose, and you weren't in control of when you came back. This is the uncomfortable part. It makes you wish you had more control. How can you prevent this from happening?

To take the mystery out of a skill, do it in slow motion. Be willing to stop. Move so slowly that you're able to stay in your body to experience every millisecond.

If there's a part of the skill that's too scary to experience, *don't do it.* Only proceed as far as you're completely comfortable. Before it starts to get uncomfortable, stop. No kidding. We don't care if you do the skill. We only care that you feel in control. You're becoming an expert at staying in control. You will learn the skill, but not if you push or hurry.

When you practice only the comfortable part over and over, feeling it as you practice, you bring more and more of your presence into your body. After a while, you have so much presence that you *want to continue.* Now you can easily remain in your body for the next part of the skill, the part you had to leave for, earlier. It's so simple.

STEP 94: THE WHEEL

If you ever find yourself practicing a skill over and over again and having to abort it at the same point every time, it's because you're skipping time on each repetition. When you continually skip time at the same point in a given skill, I call it being on The Wheel.

Your practice goes something like this. Let's use the back float as an example.

- You begin: you lie on your back.

- You feel the water holding you up.

- You float for few seconds and think to yourself, "Here I am in my back float—it's working."

- After a few more seconds, you say to yourself, "Hmm. I've been here for a while. I wonder how long this is going to last."

- Then something happens and before you know it, you're standing up.

- Now you're back at the beginning.

- You get ready to practice it again. You're not sure what made you stop or how to make it work this time, but you're going to try.

THE WHEEL

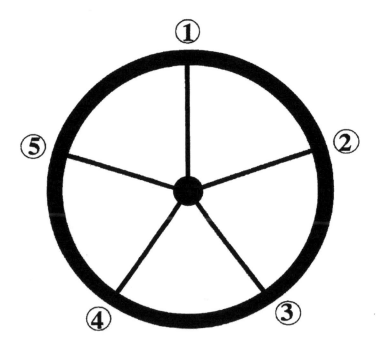

The Wheel

You go around and around this wheel until you get a new idea, or until something changes on its own. But you can have more control over it than that.

Do the skill again, and go slowly, feeling as you go, and doing only what's comfortable. Stop and back up when you need to. You'll pave a new road through the mysterious part of the skill, all the way to the end of it.

Choose a skill where you find yourself on The Wheel. Write down what your experience is at each of the five points on The Wheel above as your skill progresses, and then meets its demise. Follow the example of the back float above.

1. _____
2. _____
3. _____
4. _____
5. _____

Now, do the skill again. When you reach the point in the skill just before where it usually falls apart, slow down and feel. Examine what you're doing or thinking.
What happens?

1. _____
2. _____
3. _____

What do you need to do to shift it?

_____

_____

_____

Do that, slowly.

Confidence That's Not Quite Ripe

Margaret practiced a skill so many times that she became confident. Then she did it one more time and something went wrong. She lost it and flew out of her body to the fifth circle. This delivered her a psychic dent, to say the least.

> *"I was swimming from the deep end of the pool to the shallow end, got cold, started shivering, and panicked. Fortunately, Dennis was right there to push me toward the edge of the pool. I can't tell you how many times I have swum from one end of the pool to the other. But not this time."*

She and I discussed how to prevent this from happening again. This illustration is not about the distance or the deep water: it can be applied to any situation where confidence is not quite ripe.

Margaret was not 100% in her body during this latest practice lap. She thought she had it down, that she didn't have to go as slowly as she had in the beginning. She hadn't fully learned the skill yet. Perhaps she had mastered it 75% of the way.

If she had practiced being in her body and doing the skill slowly (she gets slower within herself the more she practices), she would have been very sensitive to the nuances of feeling cold, her balance, breath, buoyancy, air supply, and ability to propel herself. She would have been practiced at "staying here" so that if she noticed some discomfort creeping in, she could make the correction: stop, regroup, and either continue or rest…all under control. But since this hadn't happened yet, she was still vulnerable and had a moment where she scared herself.

> "You hit the nail on the head. I was definitely over-confident, not in my body or feeling. I recognize now that because of my over-confidence I did not take the time to feel before lift-off. I started to leave my body when I realized my legs were shaking so hard they were useless and that I was listing to one side, toward the middle of the pool rather than toward the shallow end. The interesting part was I kept thinking I would be okay but just needed some help. I did not even grab for Dennis. In the past I would have wrapped my arms around him in a death grip and nearly drowned both of us. I have not gone back into the deep end but have been enjoying the shallow end, doing things that are very comfortable and enjoyable. The interesting part is I feel as though I am developing new skills without trying.

What circles would you say Margaret went to? I'd say she started in the second circle, moved into the third when she realized she was shaking, and had a moment of being in the fifth. Then Dennis pushed her to the side. In the past when she put "a death grip on Dennis," it was an example of going out to the fifth circle. It took her a few months and some good conversations to heal from the episode above. Margaret is now one of our outstanding spotters.

More fun learning

STEP 95: WHAT TO DO IF YOU SCARE YOURSELF

If you scare yourself, you'll want to follow a system that will help you recover and return to trust again.

If you scare yourself, there must have been a moment, some milliseconds, when you and your body split. You may have gone only to the third circle, or out to the fifth and back. It was not fun.

You may not have realized that you had a chance to prevent your "departure." Were there any signals your body was giving you that you either didn't feel because you were *thinking* or that you dismissed?

Go over what happened in your mind. What were the thoughts just before you lost control?

_____

_____

_____

Most likely, your thoughts took you out of the present moment. You were no longer feeling what was working for you—that the water was holding you up, or that you still had enough air to survive, or that you could safely swim to the side or stand up. Did your body give you any signals that you dismissed?

_____

_____

Notice at what point in your thought process you left your body. Do you remember what your body did? _____

_____

Do you remember how you got yourself out of this?

_____

Then notice that you survived it. At least compliment yourself for that. But now you want to know how to prevent it from happening again.

Did you leave because it looked as though it was going to feel so bad that you didn't want to feel it? _____

_____

Did you leave because you forgot to go slowly?

_____

_____

I offer this: you left because you're still learning how *not* to leave. You're still learning that there's a more comfortable alternative to leaving. You haven't quite gotten it down yet, so you reverted back to an old habit. You made an inno. It's okay.

Is it okay with you? If it's not, write it out. Talk with someone who will just listen, and not try to fix it for you. You can work through this if you can just talk it through using what you're learning.

This is a moment of choice for you: do you want to hold this inno against yourself, or do you want to forgive yourself for it? Do you want to work toward mastery or stay stuck in an old pattern?

If you want to give yourself the best chance of preventing this episode from happening again, forgive yourself for it. That means you'll feel a physical letting go of the tension of holding it.

You may need to work through this a few times using the process given earlier. Give it whatever time it takes. It's worthwhile! This is what "getting back on the horse" is about. If you go about it purposely, you can have more control over your own healing.

STEP 96: YOU

THE GRACEFUL, PATIENT ARTIST

There is enjoying yourself, taking things slowly and letting them unfold on their own. This is trust.

There's enjoying yourself, taking things slowly, letting them unfold as they do on their own, seeing some things succeed beautifully and others "fail" yet staying calm and continuing to trust. This is grace.

There's the slow passing of time with no apparent advance, which lies between a belief you've held for a long time and an awaited new understanding. There's the trust that this period of confusion will clear, and the answer will be known. This is patience.

There's the euphoria of unexpectedly experiencing a miracle. This is the glorious, yet predictable reward for enjoying yourself, taking it slowly, and letting things unfold as they do on their own. This is living artfully.

Recall that part of you that has lived artfully at times in your life, even in moments today. You are no stranger to living artfully. The real you is the artist. The real you, the you that you know is you, knows that struggle is just an old habit. The real you is the graceful, patient artist.

STEP 97: REVERSALS IN THE DEEP END

Let's review the feelings of being in the deep end. Each time you go there, start from the beginning. This cannot be emphasized enough.

- Feel what it's like to be in deep water, holding onto the side.
- Notice your breathing and your internal speed.
- Allow them to be as you find them.
- If it sounds like fun, stay in the deep.
- Feel what it's like to allow your body to dangle in the deep, face in. Naturally you're holding onto the wall.
- Feel the water holding you up.
- Ask yourself if you can depend on this feeling. Can you?
- Let yourself lie backward in the water, still holding on. Review the back float at the wall.
- Feel the water holding you up.
- Ask yourself if you can depend on this feeling. Can you? How far down into your body have you gotten the belief, "I float in deep water?"

Draw a circle to show how far down into your body
you've gotten the belief, "I float in deep water."

Now, if it sounds like fun, learn to stay in your body if you let go of the deep end wall. That doesn't mean letting go of the wall and taking a chance. It's something you learn by practicing the back float and reversal in the shallow end and in the deep at the wall (even though you're holding on), being in your body so consistently that you come to accept unequivocally that the water holds you up and that you'll remain in control there with ease.

It's now incumbent upon you to give yourself this practice without scrimping. Let it be the slowest practice you have ever done. If your pool session is typically 20 minutes, let it be 20 minutes of ultra slow motion, internally and externally. Slow everything down even more than you have before.

If your energy is buzzing and you can't slow it down, so be it. Let yourself buzz. The reversal can wait for another day.

When you have practiced the back float and the reversal in the shallow water until you know beyond the shadow of a doubt that you can remain in control of it in the deep, then you'll look forward to it. It'll be safe to do it in the deep. Tell a lifeguard that you're practicing it in the deep for the first time and ask him to keep an eye on you. If it makes you self-conscious, bring yourself back into your body.

Step 98: When You're Buzzing: Your Engine Is Idling Too High

Sometimes when you get into the pool, you're buzzing from your day. Your intention is to practice. But you notice that you're vibrating so fast you can't calm down. You're speeding inside.

A useful analogy to this is an unruly car of days gone by—a car whose engine was revved up far too high. The engine was working much harder than it needed to—and it made a lot of noise doing it.

The cure for this annoyance was to use your foot to punch the accelerator quickly toward the floor and then let go so that the engine would race still higher for a moment, and then drop down to normal.

If your "engine" is idling too high and you try to practice a skill on top of that internal speed, it's easy to fly out to the 3rd or 4th circle. If you move too fast for your infrastructure to handle, you will "lose it." But there's something you can do about it. Catch yourself outside of the first circle, speeding. *Feel* the speed, which is the same as *feeling the tension*. When you feel the tension and allow it, it can begin to let go. If you continue to allow it, it will let go completely. If it is not disappearing as soon as you'd like it to, tense up more on purpose and hold onto this increased tension. Then let it go. You will drop down to a speed much slower than you were at previously.

Throughout this book we have been talking about how to be in control of your location. Now you're learning how to be in control of your speed.

STEP 99: THE CURE FOR "TOO MUCH": BUILDING INFRASTRUCTURE

When your washing machine has an unbalanced load and all the weight is on one side, the machine spins unevenly, vibrates too much, sometimes even wanders a few inches across the floor and eventually shuts down. It can't function with that much vibration. It can't handle that much energy.

When a new freeway overpass is built, inside the cement they put rebar, metal bars that give the cement added strength. The rebar enables the cement to withstand higher amounts of vibration when vehicles drive over it. Rebar is even more important if the overpass suddenly vibrates violently in an earthquake. The more rebar, the better the overpass can withstand all the energy that passes through it. Rebar adds strength and flexibility to the overpass.

When you and I are having an easy day, we can be comfortable whether we have a lot of "rebar" built inside us, or not. But when things get stressful, the more "rebar" we have, the better we respond.

I call this "rebar" infrastructure, mentioned early in the book. Infrastructure is lines of energy within our bodies, lines that we don't yet have instruments to measure but which are there that give us our ability to stay in control. These lines of infrastructure allow us to withstand large or even huge amounts of energy flowing through us, and yet still remain in control. Our "washing machine" won't shut down with an unbalanced load.

Some people have huge amounts of infrastructure—at least under certain circumstances. You'd expect a doctor to have plenty of infrastructure for the sight of blood, but the same doctor might be scared half to death in deep water.

Wouldn't it be wonderful to have tremendous infrastructure in all situations? We can build infrastructure purposefully.

Situations that test our infrastructure can be as small as being called a name when we're children. That could pull us quickly off our center and cause us to go out of balance. We may not have responded the way we wished we did.

A heavier situation could be feeling your feet sink when you're trying to learn a float in a swimming class, and thinking, "I'm sinking," then scrambling to save yourself. The situation can be anything stressful. The more stressful it is, the more infrastructure you need to remain centered and in control for it.

WHAT BUILDS NEW INFRASTRUCTURE?

- Infrastructure is confidence.
- Confidence is a feeling that you're safe.
- Feeling safe in water comes from being in control of yourself: having a choice about what to do.
- Being in control of yourself comes from being in your body, in the first circle.
- Being in the first circle allows you to be successful.
- Success builds confidence.
- Therefore, success builds infrastructure.

Put yourself into a situation where you'll be successful with your learning. Make it easy for yourself to succeed. Be gentle.

STEP 100: BOBBING WITHOUT USING THE BOTTOM

This bobbing is the act of bouncing off the water and coming up to get a breath. Doing it just once is called one "bob." Earlier you learned the chair toy and bouncing off the water. Let's review them. Use a nose clip. "Sit" in a reclined chair position with your feet on or near the bottom in shallow water. Take a small to medium breath so that you can "sit" with your face below the surface. If you're fairly buoyant, your face will be above the surface, which is fine. Extend your arms at shoulder height, just below the surface, and push downward on the water, sweeping with your "paddles" and the inside surfaces of your arms. This raises you out of the water.

Your sweep pushes you upward. Then, once you rise up as high as your sweep takes you, gravity takes over and you drop back below the surface as far down as it can take you before buoyancy takes over. You bounce off the water at the imaginary line where gravity loses its force and buoyancy takes over. Wait for this to happen. You begin to float back toward the surface without effort. As you approach the surface, ask your body when to sweep downward again with your hands and arms. When you have a sense that it's time to push down, sweep downward. This will take you above the surface so that your face is in the air.

Do this many times until you can rely on the fact that the water will push you back to the surface and your arms will bring you the rest of the way out. Come to be completely in your body for this up and down movement through the water. See how much work the water does, and how little you need to do to come up. If you're a sinker, you'll have to use more than one arm pull to return to the surface. You need not hurry them.

When you have that down (and only when you have it down), add an exhalation to the end: on your way up toward the surface, just before you come into the air, forcefully expel your air. Since you'll be wearing a nose clip, you'll exhale through your mouth.

Once your air has been forcefully expelled there will be room in your lungs to receive a new breath. If you do have room in your lungs, go ahead and take a *comfortable* breath when your head is above water. You don't have to take the biggest breath that will fit.

Just do one of these bobs at a time for now. After one, stand up. When you're ready, do the same thing again. Practice this many times.

Reminder:

Bouncing off the water and bobbing

When you've learned a skill like this, give yourself rest time afterward to absorb it. Don't move to learning another skill until you feel fresh and rested.

STEP 101: MORE TOYS

HANDSTAND

Knowing what you know now, can you do a handstand in the water? It's easier to do this in water than on land. It's easier in chest-deep water than in three feet of water.

As always, the first priority for this skill is to remain in control. Maintain comfort for your nose: use a nose clip. The game is to place your hands on the bottom of the pool with your torso aligned vertically above. Get your weight lined up vertically over your hands so that your weight drives your hands to the bottom and keeps them there.

How do you get your hands to the bottom and keep them there? Experimenting with this teaches you about buoyancy, balance and how the water works.

You need to align torso and legs vertically over your hands. First, drive your hands to the bottom. Start in a front float. Kick both feet down at the same time so that your hips come up. Bend severely (in half) at the waist. Your hands will be driven to the bottom.

Here are three steps to a handstand. Finding your own way may look different.

The end result. Your arms could also be
straight and your palms flat. Getting your weight directly over
your head is the main point. Arms and hands are just details.

Just have fun with handstands. The point isn't necessarily to do one: it's to
learn about moving your body in the water. With play, you'll get it.

SOMERSAULTS

A good toy for teaching yourself about balance and propulsion in the water is the somersault. Have you done one on land? If not, no problem.

As with all our other toys and skills, please let go of whether or not you do a "sommie" today or within a few days. The most important part of it is learning about your balance. Take it easy.

Wear a nose clip. Tuck yourself into a ball and draw your knees and head together: keep your knees and head very close together the whole time.

In a ball, head and knees close enough together

Turn yourself with your arms. Place your hands behind you, palms facing the floor. Your arms/hands are your propellers. Sweep forcefully toward the bottom with both arms/hands. Churning your propellers in large powerful circular sweeps, turn yourself completely over until you've done a 360.

Somersault

If it doesn't work, check to see if you're doing the two steps above: tuck and churn. It's common to come out of a ball, which makes a sommie nearly impossible. You may need to slow down drastically and just focus on staying in a ball.

If it still doesn't work, try again, focusing on your head position. If your head isn't aligned with your spine, you'll turn sideways.

Take your time. If there's a point at which you feel disoriented—if you and your body are out of sync—slow down to bring yourself together. Churn only as long as you feel in control. Then stop and stand up. It's okay to just go partway around.

Give yourself time to learn this. Remember, it's the journey that's most beneficial in the long run rather than completing the somersault. These games are helping you learn oneness with yourself, your body and the water.

When you master this, and other skills in this book, give yourself—or better yet, ask for—a STANDING OVATION. You certainly deserve it.

CLOSING YOUR EYES

When you wish to practice exercises in the shallow end that will help you build confidence in the deep end, you can include practicing with your eyes closed. First, master the exercises with your eyes open.

If this frightens you, it's not time to do it. You could take an intermediate step toward it, however, by closing one eye. Or, close your eyes halfway. If you do, feel your body's reaction to this and *let it be there*. Just do what is fun.

If you're ready to try it, practice closing your eyes while you do a front float. Often people say they can feel more with their eyes closed.

> **FEELING MORE IS A GREAT THING**

Spend time feeling your floats, your turns (the ball), reversal, and games, with your eyes closed. Get your feedback from feeling rather than seeing. This is fabulous practice for building your presence in each skill.

STEP 102: KNOWING WHERE THE SURFACE IS

When you roll from your back to your stomach or your stomach to your back, you need to know where the surface is so you'll know when to open your mouth for a breath and when not to. If you're in your body, you'll know. If you have been taking on water, practice this.

Roll over using a nose clip and do it slowly. Do it so slowly that you can pay attention to where your face is.

291

Be sure that:

- your first priority is to stay in control.

- your second priority is to keep your face and breath comfortable.

- your third priority is to roll over.

Once you feel at ease with these priorities, you can pay attention to where the surface is. Do you see why it's important not to skip any steps?

Before you roll, notice where the surface is relative to your head and face. As you roll, feel your face as it moves past the surface, an inch at a time. Be in your face.

Practice this over and over. When you know that your face is in the air, you'll know it's safe to open your mouth and get a breath.

STEP 103: BOUNCING OFF THE WATER IN THE DEEP

When you have learned bouncing off the water in the shallow end, you'll know it so well that you may have the thought, "If I could do this in deep water, I could get air whenever I wanted it." True.

Being able to get air when you want it is the second most important skill to have. You can't get air when you want it unless you're in your body. That is why we call *being in control* the most important skill. Do you agree?

When you've practiced being in the first circle and bouncing off the water in the shallow end—until you know beyond the shadow of a doubt that not only can you do it in the shallow, but it will work in the deep end—you may try it in the deep. It will work.

The exhalation comes a little after the downward push with your palms/inner arms. Your upward momentum will now lift you above the surface. Once your air has been forcefully expelled there will be room in your lungs to receive a new breath. If you do have room in your lungs, go ahead and take a comfortable breath when your head is above water. You don't have to take the biggest breath that will fit.

If you haven't mastered the skill in shallow water, stay there and keep practicing it. You are in charge of keeping yourself safe.

Ready for an intermediate step? Go to the deep end. Wear a nose clip. Float vertically. When you know that the water holds you up and that you can float near the wall holding your breath, practice bouncing off the water, but without the breathing. This is instructive (not to mention fun). Just sweep downward on the water, causing you to rise up above the surface. Let gravity take you back under. Let buoyancy bring you back up. Feel what's happening. If you remain in your body and continue to practice this, something will eventually come to you: the breathing. If it doesn't come on the first day, trust it. It will come when you're in your body and ready. You might go back to shallow water or crown-depth water and practice until this becomes part of you.

TREADING WATER COMES SOON

What is treading water? It's staying in one place in the water, vertically, with your feet off the bottom and your head above the surface so you can see in any direction, and talk. It's not the most restful skill you can do in the water: floating on your back is. It's not the easiest way to get air in deep water: floating on your back, and/or bouncing off the water are.

The skills that lead up to treading are far more important than treading itself, and must be learned first. Treading must be left out of this book. When you learn the skills that precede it, it's likely that you'll teach yourself to tread. Start from a comfortable vertical float, 100% in the first circle.

By the time you reach this page, you will have made vast progress in your understanding of how to overcome fear, if not also in your swimming. *Standing ovation for you.* If you have not yet gotten into the water, the fun is yet to begin. *Have a wonderful time.* Seal your book in a plastic bag, flatten it and go. Don't put your bag in the water to read off the bottom: it will just float to the top!

Many students have said that following this course has influenced their lives in many more ways than just learning to swim.

> *"A fear manifested in swimming may underlie every other aspect of one's life. The possibility that learning how to swim could eradicate fear in other parts of my life was an eye-opener for me...."*
> —Corrie

> *"Funny, since I conquered so much fear in these past two weeks, the world has opened up for me."*
> —Mary (age 71)

Hopefully, this book provides you with ideas that have already caused shifts in your thinking.

STEP 104: INVENTORY

Take stock of the beliefs and skills you have embodied, and those you still wish to acquire. Check the ones you *own.*

Beliefs

1. _____ It's safe to put my face in water.

2. _____ It's safe to go under water.

3. _____ It's okay to go at my own pace and not push myself.

4. _____ It's safe to walk to the middle of shallow water.

5. _____ I can stay in my body in shallow water for some things.

6. _____ The water holds me up in the shallow end.

7. _____ I know how long I can hold my breath.

8. _____ Shallow water is a safe place for me.

9. _____ I understand what staying in my body means.

10. _____ It's okay to be afraid in water.

11. _____ If I start to lose it, I trust myself to bring myself back to my body.

12. _____ It's possible for me to have fun in shallow water.

13. _____ Swimming is not such a mystery anymore.

14. _____ It doesn't matter where the bottom is.

15. _____ I can stay in my body in shallow water, no matter what I do.

16. _____ It doesn't matter where the side is.

17. _____ I can get a breath when I need one.

18. _____ I know which way is up and which way is down when I'm in water.

19. _____ It's okay if my feet go to the bottom when I float in shallow water.

20. _____ The water holds me up in the deep end.

21. _____ I am free in a pool.

22. _____ I can be free in deep open water.

23. _____ It's easier to learn to swim than I thought.

24. _____ There's hope for me and my swimming.

Skills
I am comfortable with these skills (not in any particular order):

1. _____ getting into the water

2. _____ walking in the water

3. _____ putting one ear in water at a time

4. _____ putting my ears in water

5. _____ putting my face in water

6. _____ relaxing my face in water

7. _____ opening my eyes under water

8. _____ smiling under water

9. _____ exhaling through my mouth into the water

10. _____ exhaling through my nose into the water

11. _____ blipping (blowing out a few bubbles of air through my nose)

12. _____ holding my breath under water

13. _____ doing a front float holding onto the side

14. _____ doing a back float holding onto the side

15. _____ doing a front float at the ladder (hands clasped behind it)

16. _____ doing a back float at the ladder (holding on loosely with one hand)

17. _____ doing a front float away from the wall

18. _____ doing a back float away from the wall

19. _____ unfloating from a front float next to the wall

20. _____ unfloating from a back float next to the wall

21. _____ unfloating from a front float in the middle of shallow water

22. _____ unfloating from a back float in the middle of shallow water

23. _____ reversals

24. _____ reversal and swim back to wall, shallow

25. _____ reversal and swim back to wall, deep

26. _____ prone float

27. _____ swimming on my back

28. _____ swimming on my front

29. _____ jumping off the bottom

30. _____ jumping into shallow water

31. _____ getting out of pool in shallow water without a ladder

32. _____ rolling from back float to front float

33. _____ rolling from front float to back float

34. _____ rolling 360 degrees (seal roll)

35. _____ staying in my body as I approach the wall

36. _____ buying a nose clip

37. _____ using a nose clip

38. _____ buying goggles

39. _____ chair toy

40. _____ knowing the difference between different hand positions

41. _____ rising above the surface from chair toy with an arm sweep

42. _____ descending a ladder and "taking the elevator" back up

43. _____ swimming in the direction of my feet when I'm on my front

44. _____ swimming in the direction of my feet when I'm on my back

45. _____ swimming in the direction of my head when I'm on my back

46. _____ swimming in the direction of my head when I'm on my front

47. _____ being in my body

48. _____ coming back to my body from the second or third circle

49. _____ not needing to return to my body because I didn't leave it

50. _____ knowing where the surface is relative to my nose and mouth

51. _____ whale jumps

52. _____ turning 360s sideways

53. _____ steering in different directions: whichever way I want to go

54. _____ checking on my location to avoid bumping into something

55. _____ going to the bottom in the shallow

56. _____ going to the bottom in the deep

57. _____ bobbing to get air, feet on bottom (shallow end breathing exercise)

58. _____ bobbing to get air, feet off bottom (chair toy)

59. _____ bobbing to get air in the deep

60. _____ keeping water out of my nose

61. _____ sitting on the bottom

62. _____ standing on the bottom in the deep

63. _____ vertical float

64. _____ bouncing off the water

65. _____ ball

66. _____ being bounced as a ball

67. _____ bouncing someone else as a ball

68. _____ hopping

69. _____ becoming balanced (after tipping)

70. _____ squirting water from my mouth (not spitting)

71. _____ swallowing under water with mouth closed

72. _____ coughing under water

73. _____ falling in from standing in the water

74. _____ falling sideways

75. _____ somersaults

76. _____ handstands

77. _____ sculling to give my body lift

78. _____ rising from the bottom using 1 or 2 arm sweeps

79. _____ rising from the bottom using just legs

80. _____ gliding after I propel myself

STEP 105: FINALE

If you've learned the main message of this book, you're to be congratulated.

If you have stayed in your body on purpose and tried anything in the book, you're to be crowned.

And if you have done everything in this book, or nearly everything, and you stayed in your body for it, you have graduated.

There is no doubt in my mind that the universal teaching in this book will succeed in overtaking any fear. Go forth and be free.

STAY WET!
And stay tuned.

I got your message: Slow down. Slow Down... no matter what I did. Even if I did well. Slow down. And somewhere in the slowing down, I got it!! I had tears of joy which were difficult to see in the water (smile). But they were there.

— Lakiba

INDEX

A

B

Breakfast: 49–50, 68

Breath / Breathing: 1, 63, 65–66, 72, 76–78, 80, 99–100, 103, 105, 117, 119, 121, 124–126, 133, 149, 154–158, 159, 179–184, 188, 217, 222, 223–226, 229–230, 250, 251, 255, 257, 265, 276, 284–285, 291–296

Buoyancy: 29, 70, 86, 92, 103–104, 113, 121, 127, 132, 135, 138, 187–188, 191, 228, 239, 248–249, 254, 276, 285, 287, 293

Buzzing: 282–283

C

Catching yourself: 80, 282

Choice: 8, 23, 42, 45, 91, 210, 263, 279, 284
    Control: xviii–2, 5, 9–20, 22–34, 39, 48–51, 55–56, 64–69, 72–73, 75–77, 79–81, 84–89, 90, 92–93, 106, 109, 111, 113, 115–116, 120–122, 125–126, 135–138, 149–150, 154, 159, 163, 171, 174–177, 180–182, 190, 193, 198, 199, 208–209, 215, 219–225, 232, 234, 240–241, 245–248, 250, 253, 255, 263, 265, 271–274, 276, 278–279, 282–285, 286, 290, 292
    You have a: 45, 91

Choosing nose clip and goggles: 88, 89

Circles: 25, 33, 145, 214, 239, 264, 277
    Five: 33

Coins: 193

Confidence: xi, 7, 8, 9, 11, 16, 35, 57, 80, 107, 149, 194, 218, 265, 276, 277, 284, 291
    As infrastructure: 35, 36, 40, 110, 226, 240, 244, 282, 283, 284
    Not quite ripe: 276

Contraction: 90, 267

Control: xviii, 1, 5, 9–20, 22–29, 31–34, 39, 48–50, 52, 56, 57, 64–66, 68, 69, 72, 75–77, 79–81, 84–89, 90–93, 94, 106, 109, 112, 113, 115, 116, 120–121, 125–126, 134–138, 149, 154, 156, 159, 163, 171, 174–177, 180–182, 190, 193, 196, 198, 199, 203, 208–209, 215, 219–221, 223–225, 232, 234, 240–241, 245–247, 250, 253, 255, 262, 263, 265, 271, 273, 274, 276, 278, 281–284, 286, 290, 292
    How to stay in: 13
    Losing: 28, 79, 209, 234, 240
    Necessity of: 79
    What does it mean to lose: 202

Coughing: 65, 71, 139, 221, 298

Crummy: 40

E

Energy: 17, 22–23, 80, 84, 86, 90–93, 103, 113, 133, 152, 205, 207, 210,
212, 258, 282, 283
As spirit: 17
Expands and contracts: 90–91, 136, 155, 211, 267
Grid: 35

Engine idling too high: 282

Exploration: 107

Eyes: xv, 1, 46, 49, 57, 75, 77, 86–87, 89, 92, 98, 170, 173, 176, 179,
222, 224, 282, 291, 296
Closing: 87, 291
Opening: 86–87, 291

F

Face: 11, 18, 29, 65, 68, 71, 75–80, 87–89, 93–95, 97–99, 102, 109, 111,
119, 122, 126, 147, 161, 169, 176, 178–184, 220–221, 228–230,
247, 254, 281, 285, 291, 294, 296

Fault: 7, 8, 212

Fronts of freedom in water: 11

G

Graduate: 63, 64

Grid, Energy   35

I

Idle. *See* Engine idling too high

Inno: 199, 202, 204, 208, 211–214, 231, 279

Instructor: 218
Care and feeding of: 218

Internal Signals: 30

J

Jell-O: 189

Joke: 84

L

Ladder: 53, 106, 122, 126–127, 243, 244, 248, 250, 251, 255, 296–297
  Free ride: 250
  Hands behind: 106–107, 118, 248, 290
  Making progress: 168
  Steps of learning: 3, 7–8, 11–12, 234–235

Learning: 90
  Five circles: 33
  Meter: 140, 165, 262
  Spiritual side of: 90
  Steps of: 234

Legs: 5, 19, 28, 80, 87, 90, 102, 132–134, 140, 151, 173–174, 227–229, 230, 287, 299

Location: 26–27, 50, 91, 173, 239, 283, 298

M

Misadventure: 31, 32

Mistakes: 196, 231

N

Neck
  you have a: 173

Nose: 1, 32, 65–66, 71, 75, 77, 79, 81, 88–90, 93–99, 115, 120, 125, 130, 135, 140, 158, 159, 167, 169, 173, 175–180, 182–185, 190, 191, 220–222, 224, 242–243, 254, 285, 286, 289, 291, 293, 296–298

Nose clip: 88, 89, 93, 96, 115, 120, 125, 130, 135, 140, 158, 159, 175–177, 178, 184, 187, 190, 191, 220–221, 224, 242, 284, 286, 289, 291, 293, 297

P

Panic: 1, 5, 7, 10, 15, 16, 19, 22, 25, 26, 28, 31, 33, 91, 134, 135, 136,
         181, 222, 234, 246
    As a habit: 15, 23
    Going from calm to: 26
    Preventing: 216

Parking on the bottom: 134–135

Pave new road: 170

Practice: 77, 80, 85, 94, 106, 116, 127, 133, 148, 159, 174, 182, 184, 187,
         190, 242, 246, 261, 269, 286, 292
    Breathing: 269
    When to proceed to the next step: 233

Presence: 11, 91, 264

Prone float: 132, 150–151, 158, 296

Pushing yourself: 39

R

Rest: xv, 1, 8, 11–13, 28, 42, 54, 61, 67, 73, 75, 105, 114, 124, 138, 149,
         172, 175, 184, 188, 194, 224, 228, 230, 241, 247–249, 258, 261,
         266, 269, 276, 285

Reversals: 229, 281

Richness of Exploration. *See* Exploration, richness of

Rolling over: 132, 158–159, 174–176, 223–224, 292
    On your back: 115, 119–122, 135, 138, 160, 172–174, 177, 224–225,
         229, 230, 256–257, 263, 273, 293
    On your front: 99, 247

Rotisserie: 159

S

Safety: 7–10, 16, 19, 23, 27, 31, 69, 174, 239, 240, 265
    What is: 10

Sculling: 258, 261

Seal rolls: 159, 175

Signature, aquatic. *See* Aquatic Signature

Sinker: 101, 125, 135, 187, 221, 250, 256–258, 285

U

Unfloat: 108–112, 116–117, 125–127, 229

Urgency: 3

W

Warm water, importance of: 29, 47–49

Wedge: 208

Whale jumps. *See* Toys, Whale jumps

Wisdom: 57, 69, 84

Y

You have a neck: 173

MORE MIRACLE SWIMMING® INFORMATION

If you have questions that fall within the scope of overcoming fear in water that have not been answered by this book, you're welcome to email them to author@conquerfear.com or send them to:

> Melon Dash/Book 1
> P.O. Box 6543
> Albany, CA 94706-0543.

I will endeavor to answer them and include those answers in later printings of the book.

This textbook is designed to provide self-discovery lessons for adults who wish to overcome fear in water and learn the basics of swimming. The progress made possible by this book is significant. Further progress is assured by working with an instructor licensed by Transpersonal Swimming Institute, which teaches Miracle Swimming and offers instructor training and licensing.

For information about our classes for adults afraid in water, please call Transpersonal Swimming Institute, LLC: 1-800-723-SWIM (7946) or visit http://www.conquerfear.com. For a discount coupon for classes, see the end pages.

For our instructional videotape or DVD that enhances and makes visual the main message of this book, please call TSI, 1-800-658-8805 or visit https://www.conquerfear.com/video.shtml. For a discount coupon, see the end pages.

For information about instructor trainings, visit http://www.conquerfear.com/instructors.shtml. For a discount coupon on trainings, see the end pages.

COUPON FOR TSI BEGINNING CLASS:

MIRACLE SWIMMING: NEW LESSONS FOR ADULTS AFRAID IN WATER

- GIVEN BY TSI HEADQUARTERS AND ITS LOCATIONS, ONLY

- 5% DISCOUNT IS FOR COURSE ONLY. NOT COMBINABLE WITH OTHER DISCOUNTS

- GO TO

  http://www.conquerfear.com/class_schedule.shtml

- TO REGISTER WITH DISCOUNT ONLINE, MENTION COUPON CODE CLDIS IN THE COMMENTS FIELD

- OR CALL: 1-800-723-7946

- FOR A LIST OF SWIM SCHOOLS CURRENTLY LICENSED TO TEACH MIRACLE SWIMMING CLASSES, GO TO
  http://www.conquerfear.com/LI.shtml

- FOR MORE INFORMATION, CONTACT SWIM@CONQUERFEAR.COM

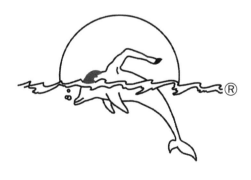

COUPON FOR TSI INSTRUCTOR TRAININGS

- FULL TRAINING WITH LICENSING: "HOW TO BE 100% SUCCESSFUL TEACHING ADULTS WHO ARE AFRAID IN WATER," (APPLICABLE TO ALL STUDENTS), DISCOUNT: $50

- PART ONE (2.5 DAY) TRAINING: "HOW TO BE 100% SUCCESSFUL TEACHING ADULTS WHO ARE AFRAID IN WATER," DISCOUNT: $25

- ONE-DAY TRAINING: FIRST STEPS TO NEW SUCCESS WITH AFRAID STUDENTS, DISCOUNT: $10

GO TO **http://www.conquerfear.com/instructors.shtml** FOR INFORMATION.

TO REGISTER ONLINE. MENTION COUPON CODE **ITDIS** IN THE COMMENTS FIELD.

FOR MORE INFORMATION, CONTACT TEACH@CONQUERFEAR.COM OR CALL: 1-800-723-7946

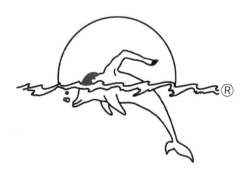

Melon Dash

Melon (M. Ellen) Dash grew up in upstate New York, but has always been a Californian at heart. She started swimming competitively when she was 7, started teaching swimming when she was 14, and has been doing both ever since. Her favorite toys are her Macintosh and her bike. She looks for a good pool to swim in, wherever she goes.

She earned her Masters degree in Education from the University of Michigan and her B.S. degree in Exercise Science and Nutrition from the University of Massachusetts/Amherst. She coached the men's and women's swim teams at Keene State College (NH) and was assistant coach of the women's teams at Harvard, University of Michigan, and University of California/Berkeley.

Miracle Swimming®

Printed in Great Britain
by Amazon